# POSTSCRIPTS

Congratulations!
You have chosen
a great Medical School.

Jeff Fisher

# POSTSCRIPTS

## For a Doctor from his Patients

Jeffrey R. Fisher, M.D., F.A.C.P.
Illustrations by Tim Janicki

JONES MEDIA
PUBLISHING

Illustrations by Tim Janicki

Jones Media Publishing
10645 N. Tatum Blvd. Ste. 200-166
Phoenix, AZ 85028
www.JonesMediaPublishing.com

Printed in the United States of America

ISBN: 978-1-945849-92-3 paperback
JMP2020.14

# DEDICATION

FOR MY DEAR WIFE,
DIANA L. VANGELLOW, BSN, RN

Who encouraged me to write these stories years ago and has
been at my side ever since.

Every two souls are absolutely different. In friendship or in
love, the two, side by side, raise hands together to find what
one cannot reach alone.
Kahlil Gibran

# CONTENTS

INTRODUCTION . . . . . . . . . . . . . . . . . . . . . . . . . . . . . . . . . . . . . . . . . 1

ZORA-MARIE THIBIDEAUX. . . . . . . . . . . . . . . . . . . . . . . . . . . . . . . 6

ROOSEVELT MCGEE. . . . . . . . . . . . . . . . . . . . . . . . . . . . . . . . . . . 15

MAC, LIBBY, AND HUCK . . . . . . . . . . . . . . . . . . . . . . . . . . . . . . . 22

JARVOUS WASHINGTON . . . . . . . . . . . . . . . . . . . . . . . . . . . . . . . 32

HOSTEEN BISCHITTY. . . . . . . . . . . . . . . . . . . . . . . . . . . . . . . . . . 40

THE WOMAN WITH NO NAME . . . . . . . . . . . . . . . . . . . . . . . . . . 49

POLINGAYSI QOYAWAYMA. . . . . . . . . . . . . . . . . . . . . . . . . . . . . 55

TROY BYLAS . . . . . . . . . . . . . . . . . . . . . . . . . . . . . . . . . . . . . . . . . 63

GREGORI LAZARASHVILI . . . . . . . . . . . . . . . . . . . . . . . . . . . . . . 69

STANISLAUS KOWALCZWYK . . . . . . . . . . . . . . . . . . . . . . . . . . . . 77

GINA ROLLEFSON. . . . . . . . . . . . . . . . . . . . . . . . . . . . . . . . . . . . . . . . . . .85

LEONARD SANTOS & CAROLYN NICHOLS

LEONARD . . . . . . . . . . . . . . . . . . . . . . . . . . . . . . . . . . . . . . . . . . . . . .92

CAROLYN. . . . . . . . . . . . . . . . . . . . . . . . . . . . . . . . . . . . . . . . . . . . . .98

GILBERT TAFOYA . . . . . . . . . . . . . . . . . . . . . . . . . . . . . . . . . . . . . . . .102

SIDNEY RHEINSTEIN . . . . . . . . . . . . . . . . . . . . . . . . . . . . . . . . . . . .109

ROBERT J. FISHER. . . . . . . . . . . . . . . . . . . . . . . . . . . . . . . . . . . . . . .116

FRANKLIN WOODY. . . . . . . . . . . . . . . . . . . . . . . . . . . . . . . . . . . . . .127

BIOGRAPHIES . . . . . . . . . . . . . . . . . . . . . . . . . . . . . . . . . . . . . . . . .133

ACKNOWLEDGEMENTS . . . . . . . . . . . . . . . . . . . . . . . . . . . . . . . . . . .135

# INTRODUCTION

A postscript is an added remark at the end of a letter, after the signature, abbreviated "P.S." Very few of my patients ever wrote me a letter, and I can recall none with a postscript. On the other hand, during my career as a doctor I've written thousands of prescriptions for my patients. In medical slang, "script" is used as a shortened version of prescription. Now retired and reflecting back over forty-five years of medical practice, I realize in many cases my patients were actually treating and educating me by their examples of courage, humor, faith, love, kindness, fortitude, and flexibility. They were giving me these "scripts" after I had rendered care for them—postscripts.

Some of these postscripts can be found in the following stories. If a doctor listens carefully to a patient's complaints, watching body language, and placing the medical history in the context of a patient's culture, this will frequently lead to the source of their problem, a diagnosis. Patients' stories not only inform attentive listeners about a patient's condition, but at times will cause listeners to realize a patient has qualities, abilities, or life circumstances that have lessons to teach us. We share feelings and experiences at the core of human life. I've written this book not as a memoir but as a way to encourage students now in medical school to consider the rewards of a career in primary care. The following stories are also meant to honor the memory of these patients and countless others that have made my career so enjoyable. Some of the names have been changed for reasons of privacy and respect. The events I relay are accurate to the best of my memory.

Although not as financially rewarding as some specialties, there is a great need in the United States for doctors in family practice, pediatrics, and internal medicine—now called "primary care providers"—especially in urban and rural settings. Some medical schools, including my alma mater, have recognized this need and are developing programs to forgive student loans and award financial incentives to students selecting programs in primary care.

Before I chose to specialize in internal medicine as a third-year medical student, I still considered a surgical career. It seemed glamorous and I liked the surgeons' can-do approach. But those early aspirations dramatically changed one morning in an operating room during a rotation in orthopedic surgery. Sometimes the hand of fate helps with our decisions.

The Columbia Presbyterian Medical Center draws dignitaries from around the world: kings, presidents, the famous come from many countries to be evaluated and treated, as do the residents of New York City and Washington Heights, the neighborhood that surrounds the medical center. In 1967, the granddaughter of Papa Doc Duvalier, the ruthless and autocratic president of Haiti, was brought to New York to be treated by Dr. Frank Stinchfield, a world authority and pioneer in hip replacement surgery. Mademoiselle Duvalier suffered from congenital dysplasia of her right hip and limped with pain until age sixteen, when she was sent by her father to Dr. Stinchfield for surgery. She was accompanied by two large Haitian bodyguards, members of the Tonton Macoutes, Papa Doc's private militia, who stationed themselves outside the doors of the operating room armed with automatic weapons. The medical center and New York City itself was on high alert. An assassination attempt or a kidnapping would be disastrous. The only glitch in security was in the selection of the medical student admitted to the operating room.

This was my first time in an operating suite. I had studied the relevant anatomy of the hip and had received instruction in accepted operating room procedures: hand washing, gowning, gloving, the need to be quiet and follow instructions from the surgeon. My sole responsibility was to support the ample right leg of Mademoiselle Duvalier during surgery. That seemed easy enough. I was fully gowned and gloved. A nurse pinched the metal stay in the face-mask around the bridge of my nose so that my eyeglasses wouldn't fog during surgery. I had not been instructed, however, in the proper method of securing the pants of my scrub suit. This was probably considered to be in the realm of common sense and not a necessary part of the medical school curriculum, but it's always the little things in life— the rivets on the Titanic, a few insulation tiles on the Space Shuttle, the lack of a dry match in the Canadian North—that lead to bigger problems.

Normally, one retracts the cotton material from the drawstring before tying the scrub pants. In a hurry, and probably absentmindedly, I had tied the cotton material of the pants and the cord together in a bunch. As a consequence, during surgery the waistband loosened and my pants headed south. Not wishing to be depantsed during my first opportunity in the OR, I spread my legs apart. In so doing, I accidentally stepped on the pedal of the Bovie, an instrument used to coagulate small blood vessels during surgery. The instrument itself resembles a wood burning tool familiar to most Cub Scouts. There was a high pitched hum in the background, but as this was my first time in the OR, the sounds were all new to me—the pumping of the anesthesia compressor, the click of instruments, suction devices, bone saws. Before long, however, the anesthesiologist became alarmed: "Holy shit, the drapes are on fire!"

Sure enough, smoke and a small flame issued from the drapes between the generous thighs of Mademoiselle Duvalier. Dr. Stinchfield sized up the situation quickly and decisively: "Get the damn medical student out of here!" I cannot repeat the rest of his comments. The first-year orthopedic resident took possession of the patient's leg and gave me a hip check, probably learned in prep school and later perfected on the Yale varsity hockey team. Humiliated, I headed for the operating room exit, my legs wide apart like a western gunslinger, my pants still problematic. It seemed clear at the time that a surgical career was not likely to be in my future.

Thinking back, I should have recognized earlier signs I was not destined to become a surgeon. For example, the cadavers in gross anatomy were assigned to four students, two working in partnership on each side of the pickled body. I worked with Don Feinfeld. Eric

Frisbee and Richard Framer dissected the other side. Fisher and Feinfeld's side looked like ground round; we chose internal medicine. Frisbee and Framer became successful surgeons. Their dissection looked like a page from the anatomy textbook. Things often work out for the best after all.

They have for me. I've been fortunate to have a profession that offers new challenges each day. I enjoy the process of diagnosing an illness and then establishing a long-term partnership with a patient to manage their condition. What better way to spend the day than listening to stories and witnessing the boundless variety of strengths, insights, and coping skills of patients who allow the doctor to be a trusted presence in their lives. It is my hope that these stories will encourage medical students to explore the unique relationships that can develop between doctor and patient. They then will find an abundance of stories and experiences of their own.

# Zora-Marie Thibideaux

Sweat dissolved the starch from my white hospital uniform. The heat and humidity were so oppressive on that August night, I imagined that even the snakes on the Staff of Caduceus, symbol of the medical profession, embroidered in red on the shoulder of my jacket, would slither off to seek cooler refuge. Conditions were even more unbearable on the airless fifth floor hallway of this Harlem tenement house, but the scene before me was so unreal, so horrible, that I was transfixed and forgot my physical discomfort. Down the hallway, less than 20 feet away, was an elderly African-American woman who appeared to weigh more than 500 pounds. She was sitting motionless in an equally enormous red velour armchair. A purple tongue protruded through swollen lips, mocking those who had arrived too late. Her legs and feet were so edematous that serous fluid blistered the dark skin of her feet and ankles, soaking an oversized pair of worn pink house slippers that barely covered her swollen feet. A loose cotton print dress draped her body like a floral parachute, the pattern obscuring a leather gris-

gris bag hanging from her neck. Milky brown eyes, wide open, startled by death, stared for eternity at the lead paint peeling from the hallway ceiling. A Japanese paper fan rested in her lap.

That woman died in 1969 when I was an intern at Harlem Hospital Center, a teaching hospital of Columbia University where I had done several rotations during the last two years in medical school. A war was being fought in Vietnam but also on the streets of America. Riots destroyed the Watts neighborhood of Los Angeles in 1965, the same year that Malcolm X was assassinated. The Audubon Ballroom, where Malcolm X said "Asalaikum, brothers and sisters" for the last time, was only thirty blocks away from where I stood. Five days of arson, looting, and rioting paralyzed Detroit in 1967. One year later Martin Luther King was gunned down on the balcony of the Lorraine Motel in Memphis.

Racial tensions were peaking when construction of the new tower at Harlem Hospital Center was completed. Critically ill patients had to be transferred from the ancient brick hospital built in 1907 to the modern glass and steel complex next door. Emergency services could not be disrupted; there was too much at stake. Mayor John Lindsay, well aware of the political and racial tensions, directed medical interns to ride in the ambulances during the week of transition to the new hospital. I was assigned to ride the midnight to eight shift, but, as a new doctor, I was just window dressing for the mayor. Sure, I could start a central line, intubate an airway, and stop bleeding, but the real pros, the ones in charge, were the ambulance driver, Malcolm Little, and medic, Leroi Bonlieu. We were all about the same age, in our mid to late 20s, and quickly bonded like combat soldiers in a trench. Even Malcolm and Leroi had only been working the ambulance for less than a year and were not yet hardened or indifferent to the misery and suffering, the squalor, violence, and abandonment written on the buildings with graffiti and etched on the tormented faces of our patients trapped in this dark place.

Leroi, an extrovert, suggested we take nicknames—less formal. He spoke with a distinctive Cajun voice: "I'm Leroi Bonlieu, that's French for 'King of the Good Place', so I be the King. Now Malcolm, he be Malcolm Little, same as Malcolm X 'fore he changed his name. We call you X, okay Malcolm?" Always quiet and reserved, Malcolm nodded with a wry smile. "Now, lemme see," he looked at my name plate: J. Fisher, M.D. "Doc, how 'bout we call you Dr. J, you know like Julius Erving of the 76ers." I told him that would be fine. I admired Julius Erving as a basketball player and as a person.

So there we were: the King, X, and Dr. J. That first night together Leroi showed me the ambulance layout and our inventory of emergency supplies. Everything seemed in order, but there were some items that I was surprised to find. Switchblade knives were strapped to the calves of both the King and X. In addition, they carried a loaded .45 caliber handgun in the emergency bag. The weapons were clearly not standard issue from New York City Department of Hospitals, but both the King and X assured me that they might be useful, even necessary. They'd been around.

Until this assignment, I had been naively comfortable in the neighborhood. I often walked three blocks from the hospital to catch the A train subway back to the medical school, usually after dark. I wore a Timex watch that no one would steal, and carried little money. I stepped around the garbage, dog excrement, and an occasional homeless person asleep on the sidewalk. Even the few times that I was stopped by panhandlers, neighbors seeing my white hospital uniform would yell from windows or from across the street, "Leave our doctor alone!" At the time I was reminded of a story about Arnold J. Toynbee, the world-renowned Oxford professor of history who taught for a year at Columbia University. Professor Toynbee had always carried a British ten pound sterling note in his jacket pocket. In New York, he carried the equivalent, a twenty dollar bill, in case he was ever accosted by thugs. When he was 72 years old he ultimately was stopped by hoods. Professor Emeritus Toynbee, surprised and incensed, beat them off with his cane, hobbled into his apartment, and locked the door, still in possession of the twenty dollars. I guess we can never predict our reactions until we are confronted face-to-face with danger.

Most of the week, riding in the ambulance was an adrenalin charged experience: overdoses, shootings, stabbings, heart attacks, epileptic seizures, asthmatic and insulin reactions. Between calls the three of us often sat on the hydraulic lift on the back of our ambulance van parked on top of the gentle downslope of 141$^{st}$ Street, drinking from Malcolm's bottomless thermos of coffee or passing around Havana cigars sent to Leroi from his brother-in-law in Tampa. It was our first night on duty that I recall best. A dispatch came in: "Female, respiratory distress, 158th Street and Lenox." Leroi gave what became his traditional Cajun response: "Laissez les bon temps rouler!" (Let the good times roll). This would be my first time inside a tenement building.

Even in the palpitating rush to that first emergency, events seemed to move in slow motion. I can recall the smallest details. The lobby floor was tiled with black and white hexagons—black and white like us; little hexagons familiar to medical students from their study of organic chemistry. The hexagons together formed a pattern like honeycomb, symbolic of the entrance to a foreboding giant human hive that we were about to enter. A neon bulb buzzed overhead and bathed the entrance with an eerie ultraviolet hue. In front of us was an open staircase that ascended seven floors deeper into the hive. Crying and screaming came from above. Leroi told Malcolm and me to stay put and wait by the door. He looked up the staircase for shooters or jumpers. This place was from a different world: babies screeching, domestic quarrels exploding, the hum of traffic and rumble of the subway from two blocks away, the tempo of Motown beating from multiple radios, and boom boxes like cardiac contractions from a single giant organism. The building reeked of stale beer, urine, cooking pork fat, and cigarettes. A used diaper, discarded plastic syringes, a newspaper, and an empty cardboard bucket from Colonel Sanders littered the space next to the stairs. Then the King motioned to us that the coast was clear. Up the stairs we went, X dragging the stretcher and me carrying the emergency kit—adrenalin, Narcan, bandages, scissors, ACE wraps, endotracheal tubes, catheters, a tracheostomy set, and, of course, the .45 caliber handgun.

On the fifth floor we found her. The enormous dead woman slumped in the red velour armchair. She had no pulse or respiration; her pupils were fixed and dilated. Standing beside her was a skinny, short man with graying hair—a single drone with the queen. Apparently, the man spoke little English. He kept pleading with the woman, "Reveiller, Cher' Tit Chou" (Wake up dear, wake up). The man told us that she kept her chair in the hallway where it was cooler than in her tenement flat. Also, she was much more accessible to her many visitors. "Maman a rendu service et a donne conseil a là demande" (Maman was always available to give advice or help). The man could barely get these words out, he was so unsettled.

Leroi was professional, but I sensed that he was upset, perhaps by the profound despair of the man. There was some unusual hesitancy as he gently touched the woman's neck to feel for a carotid pulse and then softly closed each eyelid after checking her pupillary reflexes. Suddenly he seemed to snap back to the business at hand. She was too big to move. We might drop her. The King decided that we should strap her chest and waist to the chair and then affix the chair to the stretcher. With emergency ropes, we belayed her down the stairs like an alpine mountain rescue. The King led, and X, with his huge muscular arms, braced the rope from above. I watched and carried our equipment. Then I noticed a change. Something was different. The building became silent. Men, women, and children began to fill the hallways and gather along the railings of each floor, respectfully watching the macabre procession of the dead woman in her chair known to all of them, an enthroned black queen attended by three workers, one white, two black. Some of the bystanders, now a swarm, lit candles. Some made the sign of the cross. Along the descent down the five floors to the street level, neighbors kissed their fingertips and then touched the woman's lips. Some hung rosaries around her stout neck. Others placed objects in her lap next to the Japanese fan: picture cards of saints, a goat's ear, tobacco, a small bottle of dark rum, a smooth black stone, straight pins, what looked like a mummified umbilical cord, a letter. Outside, on the street, word had apparently spread. A murmuration of people lined the curbs. The King and X placed the woman and her chair on the hydraulic lift and removed the gurney. As she ascended slowly into the humid air of that Harlem night her head bobbed slightly as if to acknowledge the well wishers. There were voices calling, "Adieu, Maman. Je t'aime. Bless you, Maman. God be with you, Maman Zora."

We drove slowly and silently back to the hospital, our red ambulance lights flashing against the surrounding tenement buildings. The dead woman strapped to her red chair sat bolt upright behind us in the ambulance, her features intermittently illuminated by the pulses of red light. After driving a few blocks Leroi cleared his throat and explained the events of this bizarre emergency call. He had known the elderly woman since he was a little boy in Baton Rouge, Louisiana. She was his mother's best friend. When Leroi's father abandoned the family, his mother moved to New York with Leroi and his two sisters where his mother had relatives to help raise the children. This woman moved with them from Baton Rouge to New York.

Her name was Zora-Marie Thibideaux, but everyone called her "Maman"—mother. Originally from Haiti, she moved to Louisiana as a young woman to marry her first husband. She was a voodoo priestess, a fortune teller, a healer, and a friend to many. Zora lived in the same Harlem appointment for the last 48 years. If anyone needed a temporary job or a work excuse, Maman knew where to call. If there was a colicky baby or a teething infant, Maman knew the right herbal remedy. If a boyfriend ran around behind your back, Maman knew just where to place the pin in her voodoo doll to inflict maximum suffering. She conversed with the dead and went into trances to predict the future with remarkable accuracy. The small man at her side was only her most recent Haitian boyfriend. Maman Zora-Marie Thibideaux had outlived three husbands. She was both loved and feared by those who knew her. She was kind, wise, caring, mystical, and spiritual. She lived on the generosity of those she helped, refusing welfare or government assistance. Nonetheless, those who crossed Maman often developed unexplained health problems or just disappeared.

In the years to come, I often reflected on that August evening in 1969, especially on the great outpouring of love and respect shown to Maman. I was often frustrated when my patients wouldn't follow my advice, take their medicine correctly, keep follow-up appointments, or adhere to their diets. They wouldn't listen to me; I was just a young white doctor. My patients at Harlem had known me for only a year or two. Besides, I didn't know where to place a pin to punish a wayward boyfriend, how to converse with the dead, or how to predict the future. I realized that after four years of medical school, I really didn't know much about the needs of my patients after all. Even without the challenge of treating patients from a different culture, compliance with my advice was often challenged until I'd spent months, even years, with some patients. Trust came only after a patient believed that I cared about them as an individual, listening to their needs and expectations. After that night I began to understand that good doctoring takes patience and respect and time. It requires a special bonding between doctor and patient, a community of two, sharing in the life and culture of the larger community of family, friends, and neighbors. Merçie, Maman Zora. Adieu, et bon voyage.

# ROOSEVELT McGEE

During my years in medical school in the 1960s, a transition was made after the second year when cadavers, rats, petri dishes, and microscopic slides were replaced by instruction from real patients. Today, students are introduced to patient care earlier in their training, combined with instruction in the basic sciences. Most of my clinical rotations were at the Columbia Presbyterian Medical Center, but we also could choose clerkships at other New York hospitals where the Columbia University faculty held teaching positions (St. Luke's, Roosevelt, Belleview, and Harlem). I chose many of my clerkships at Harlem Hospital Center, where the teaching staff was excellent and where patients presented with a diversity of acute and chronic illnesses. It was there I was instructed in cardiology, nephrology, neurology, and infectious disease. At Harlem Hospital I was also instructed by a man who would affect my career more than either of us knew at the time. . .

Roosevelt McGee was born in South Carolina, but moved to New York City as a young man where he established a career selling shoes. When I met him, he was in his late 60s and ravaged by diabetes, congestive heart failure, and moderately advanced kidney disease. He was prescribed a complex regimen of medications to lower his blood sugar, regulate his heart rate and fluid balance, and control his cholesterol and blood pressure. His vision was failing, and the sensation in his feet was decreased due to diabetic neuropathy. When we first met he was less than compliant taking medication and rarely followed dietary restrictions, but he always had a smile and a good word for everyone in the clinic. He often expressed admiration for my neckties, as did many of the staff and patients. I got them at Tie City, a unique store near Times Square. For a dollar each, Tie City's neckties came in a kaleidoscope of colors and an extraordinary array of patterns: tie-dye, flowers, plaids, stripes, paisleys, animal prints—they made Sgt. Pepper's outfits look funereal. The enthusiasm for my ties gave me an idea. I was a young white doctor, and I needed to earn my patients' trust. Maybe I could use the ties as an incentive—well, okay, a bribe. Good attendance and compliance for three consecutive visits and a patient could choose a tie. Extra ones were awarded for good behavior during a hospital stay. During the three years I knew Roosevelt McGee, he was the recipient of fifteen neckties.

It was toward the end of my internship that Mr. McGee had a serious hospitalization caused by lobar pneumonia. I was making hospital rounds on a Sunday afternoon and he was recovering. When I finished seeing my other patients, I returned to his bedside. We sat and drank coffee for a while. He loved to talk. The only negative words I ever heard from Mr. McGee concerned my footwear. I favored closed-toe sandals with socks as my feet perspire, and I am more comfortable with open shoes. He considered my choice of footwear highly unprofessional, a disgrace to the medical profession. "Doc, you gotta have some pride, some self-respect. How you gonna ax your patients to lissen to you dressed like a bum, like some hippie? Doan ya know dat of all de clothes God gives us, it de shoes dat tells mos 'bout de man?" Then Mr. McGee told me a story he learned from a Cuban grocer. Cuban mothers tell their daughters to spill coffee on their boyfriend's shoes to see how they react. That's how the boyfriend will treat the girl after they've been together for a while. Mr. McGee added, ever the dedicated shoe salesman, "Now dat's good advice. Doze Cuban men, dey luv dair shoes."

We sat sipping coffee from Styrofoam cups, listening to piano music and singing voices that echoed into Mr. McGee's hospital room from the dayroom down the hallway. The choir from New Pilgrim Way Baptist Church came every Sunday. Mr. McGee was a deacon at the church. Gospel voices sang: "Oh Happy Day"; "When Jesus Walks"; "Jesus Lover of My Soul"; "Down by the Riverside." It was then, sitting at Mr. McGee's bedside, I noticed a Mason jar containing an odd substance on his nightstand.

Roosevelt McGee told me the jar contained dirt from his farm in South Carolina. He carried it everywhere. His grandfather had been captured by slave traders on the Ivory Coast of Africa and brought to America in a slave ship. He survived the arduous journey, but his wife and two sons were not so fortunate. They died of dysentery and were thrown overboard. Years later, in America, his grandfather found a new wife. They worked on a plantation near the present-day town of Buford, South Carolina. When the plantation slaves received their freedom, each adult was given ten acres of land. It was on those combined twenty acres inherited from his grandparents that Mr.

McGee's father and mother raised him with his three brothers and two sisters. He was told as a child his grandfather scraped his fingernails in African soil as he was dragged to the slave ship. It was only after his arrival in America that he took a splinter of wood from the old barn and dug the African soil from beneath his nails, mixing it with the rich plantation earth of South Carolina. It was this soil, a blend from two continents, that was contained in Mr. McGee's glass jar.

But Roosevelt McGee was not a farmer. He was a businessman, an entrepreneur. By age fourteen, he had organized a cooperative of Black farmers that sold fresh produce, at a fair price, to the White residents of Buford, South Carolina. He later traded ten pigs for two dairy cows and used the milk to make a special cheese, which he sold at a premium. He maintained eight beehives, sold rich magnolia honey, and shined the shoes of his customers while they waited. All the profits from these enterprises, of course, were given to his mother and father to help support the family. "I was a good boy, but I wasn't no farmer. I hated all that chicken shit and pig mud, everyone dressed in overalls, work shirts, and straw hats. Dat not the life I see for ol' Roosevelt McGee, no sir." It was the customer's shoes, the ones he shined, that captured his interest. He didn't own a pair of his own shoes until he was seven. He loved the smell and feel of fine leather, and wanted big city shoes, not work boots or canvas sneakers. At age eighteen, he said goodbye to his parents, brothers, sisters, and relations in Buford, and moved to New York City with his jar of dirt. He carried it everywhere with him for the next fifty years.

When Mr. McGee arrived in New York, he began a profitable business selling shoes from a stall on a street corner. His business skills, honed in South Carolina, worked just as well in New York City. After a few years he was able to purchase his own shoe store. Many African-American men in those days gained pride and respect from their clothing—especially from their footwear. Roosevelt McGee was no exception and relished the shine and smell of rich, imported leather. The one time I visited his store I began to share some of his enthusiasm. Upon opening the front door of Mr. McGee's establishment I was immediately rewarded by the aroma of fine leather and polish. It was better than the smell of the leather seats of a new car. And such variety: kiltie loafers, wingtips, Cuban heel dress boots, Oxfords. Many were in imported exotic leathers from Italy and North Africa: calfskin, lizard, snake, alligator, suedes, and cordovans. I did begin to share his enthusiasm, but I didn't make a purchase. I still was more comfortable in my sandals. In Mr. McGee's view, I degraded my manhood and profession.

I knew Mr. McGee for three years, two from medical school and one from internship. I enjoyed that leisurely Sunday afternoon sipping coffee in Mr. McGee's hospital room, listening to the gospel choir and learning about the mysterious jar of dirt. The next day was a rainy, cool March morning. When I exited the elevator on the medical ward, head nurse, Ramona Streets, and her aide, Lawanda Moore, were in a somber mood. Ms. Streets picked up a box and told me to follow her into the dayroom, the one with the piano where the choir had sung the day before. They told me Mr. McGee had died in his sleep during the night. His wife and two daughters had already claimed his few possessions and the jar of dirt, but this box had been left for me. I remembered one of the hymns: "Gonna Lay Down My Burden, Down By the Riverside…" Roosevelt McGee had laid all of his burdens down and had left something behind for me. I opened the box. Inside was a note: "Doctor, you de bess doctor. You be my doctor. But in some ways you lacking. I hope de contents of dis box give you some dignity." In the box was a pair of brown leather dress shoes. They fit me perfectly. Mr. McGee must have been studying my feet with a professional eye during our visits together. In one of the shoes was a business card:


ROOSEVELT MCGEE

MENS' LEATHER FOOTWARE

620 AMSTERDAM AVENUE

NEW YORK, NY

"YOU DO THE WALKIN'

LET YOUR SHOES DO THE TALKIN'"

From a man of little formal education, his message was profound and lasting. From the jar of dirt: Remember who you are and where you come from. From the gift of shoes: The kindness of a gift given from the heart lasts with the receiver forever. From the business card: Live your beliefs, don't talk about them.

I wore those brown leather shoes to my wedding and on special occasions for the next fifteen years. I continue to wear my sandals to work, however. Otherwise, Mr. McGee, my conduct and demeanor remain highly professional.

# MAC, LIBBY, AND HUCK

The first year of medical school is not the optimum time to begin a new hobby, but during my first year in medical school in New York, I became an avid birdwatcher (or birder, now the preferred term).

Manhattan has some spectacular urban spaces for birding: Riverside, Van Cortlandt, and Fort Tryon Parks, and, of course, the city's jewel, Central Park, where I met three people who changed my perspective on birds—and life.

Donald Huckabee appeared on a cool, misty Sunday afternoon in October. I'd been at the Cloisters, a replica of a 13th century monastery that houses the Metropolitan Museum of Art's priceless collection of medieval paintings, altarpieces, chalices, and tapestries. On Sundays, Gregorian chants echo through the monastery and out into the gardens overlooking the Hudson River below. I was in a bit of a spiritual trance walking back to the subway when I saw a tall young man about my age, built like a long-distance runner. He was dressed in sandals, cargo shorts, and a T-shirt that identified him as a member of the Stanford University cross-country team. A pair of binoculars hung from his neck. He seemed quite animated while gently cupping what appeared to be an exotic bird between his hands. He told me he just captured a blue-headed parrot which he had found shivering in the lower branches of a chestnut tree. Bubbling with California enthusiasm, he had been scouting Ft. Tryon Park for Eastern bird species to add to his life list. (Many birders keep lists of the number of species they identify during their lifetimes. This is called a life list.) The blue-headed parrot was unexpected, definitely not included in *Peterson's Field Guide to Eastern Birds*. Tomorrow was his wife's birthday—some present!

He asked if I enjoyed birds. I told him I liked being out of doors, had a general fondness for animals, had seen Alfred Hitchcock's movie, but had no special interest in birds themselves. "Do you have a pen and paper? Sorry, I can't shake hands, kind of tied up with this parrot. I'm Donald Huckabee. Call me Huck. Let me give you my phone number and address, just in case you ever want to see some cool birds—well, maybe not this cool," he said as he looked at the parrot. I took his address and phone number, thanked him, and told him I hoped his wife enjoyed her birthday present. I later discovered Huck had been an avid birder since he was a teenager. He was studying for a PhD in Asian studies at Columbia University, but went birding as often as his studies and his wife, Judy, permitted. I kept his phone number and address, but didn't call back for about six months. I was engrossed with anatomy, pathology, microbiology, histology, and statistics, and I preferred not to flunk out of medical school, especially during the first year.

One Saturday morning the following April, I got up early to explore Central Park. I was sitting alone on a park bench, enjoying the blossoming dogwood and azaleas, when I became aware of a woman standing about ten feet to my left, looking at the boating pond through binoculars. She appeared to be in her late 70s, dressed in a pink sundress, sensible brown shoes, and a wide-brimmed straw hat. Then she began speaking to me with a pronounced southern drawl as if I were an old friend or neighbor, while still gazing through her binoculars. This doesn't happen often, and perhaps less often in New York City. "Don't you love it right here (*lahave it riot hyear*) in the springtime? I admire the pied-billed grebe, so plucky and compact, and the way he dives on a sudden whim just like we girls used to do at Emerald Lake in Tupelo, so spontaneous and full of life." She put down her binoculars. "I'm sorry, I didn't introduce myself. I'm Elizabeth Coffee, but most everyone up here in New York just calls me Libby. Do you adore birds?" That was the second time I had been asked that question by a New Yorker, but before I could respond she mentioned, not without some irony, that her favorite book was *To Kill a Mockingbird*. She talked on and on, a monologue from a Southern belle.

Libby told me she was raised in Mississippi, married a banker from a family of wealth, moved to New York, and then after five years, was widowed. She lived in an elegant three-story brownstone on Central Park West. I knew more about this woman in two minutes than I knew about some of my own relatives. What was unusual about her, however, was not her forward manner or southern accent, but her color. Elizabeth Coffee was blue—blue like a blue-gray gnatcatcher, blue like a pale scrub jay. I later discovered she had argyria, a rare affliction resulting from the absorption of silver into the bloodstream and later deposited in the skin after repeated use of the drug Argyrol, a product used to treat ear infections in children. I recall my own mother treating me with this liquid, warmed in a saucepan and irrigated into my inflamed ear canal with a rubber bulb syringe. The skin discoloration occurs only if the drug was used frequently and over a period of years; it is striking and irreversible. Of course, Argyrol has since been removed from the market.

Then Libby continued, "I'm sorry, I didn't ask your name—Oh, Jeffrey? A distinguished name. Have you seen the warblers?" I could barely distinguish a sparrow from a pigeon, but her enthusiasm was so infectious I agreed to follow this eccentric blue woman along the wooded side of the pond. We stopped. She handed me her binoculars and pointed to a branch high in an elm tree. I was startled. In sharp focus and in the same field of view were two birds of spectacular coloration: male Blackburnian and chestnut-sided warblers, promptly identified by a field guide Libby produced from a canvas bag. Then she gave me her address and phone number. It seemed prophetic: two outgoing, enthusiastic, if somewhat unconventional New York residents giving their phone numbers to me, a complete stranger. Later that evening I called Huck. Yes, he remembered me. His wife, Judy, loved the parrot and kept it in an antique brass birdcage. Of course he'd join us in Central Park next weekend. Then I called Libby. It was a deal. We would meet in front of the Museum of Natural History the following Saturday at six a.m.

Here, I should briefly tell any non-birders that warblers don't warble. Their calls are more like high-pitched radio static. They are small, pocket-sized, nervous birds with striking coloration that hop nonstop from branch to branch eating insects to fuel their rapid metabolism. Weighing about as much as a dry peach pit, these little high-octane feather puffs migrate thousands of miles from their winter homes in South or Central America to their breeding grounds in the United States and Canada. Even their names capture our imagination: Blackburnian, prothonotary, hermit, mourning, worm-eating, myrtle, colima, parula, cerulean, bay-breasted. There are 54 species of wood warblers regularly found in North America. Furthermore, New York's Central Park is the perfect place to find them. Seen from the air—a bird's-eye view—the park is a rectangular green postage stamp midway up the concrete envelope of Manhattan Island. It's a leafy oasis, 843 acres of natural tranquility surrounded on all four sides by the cacophony of urban bustle. Migrating songbirds naturally congregate here to feed and rest before continuing their journey northward. During early spring mornings the park is alive with birders as diverse as the city itself: students from Columbia, NYU, and Union Theological Seminary in jeans and T-shirts; wives of investment bankers with pearls and white cotton gloves ushered from their Fifth Avenue apartments by doormen; laborers and clerks still in uniform, ending the night shift—all with binoculars and field guides to see the birds. Also there, of course, are the vagrants, the homeless, an infantry of the indigent, creeping with stealth from the underbrush with their few worldly possessions—a blanket, half an orange, dentures, an extra pair of socks—awakened early by the exaltations of enthusiastic birders.

Libby and Huck arrived promptly at six a.m. with their binoculars and field guides. I had borrowed a pair of mother-of-pearl opera glasses from a classmate. After brief introductions and greetings, we entered the park. Then, just a few minutes later, our path was blocked by an older man with long, unkempt hair, a filthy overcoat, ripped corduroy pants that ended well above his bare ankles, and black high-top shoes. We expected a request for a handout, but instead he said, "Have you seen the Cape May or Wilson's yet?" We looked at each other, shrugged our shoulders, and told him to lead the way. He guided us not only to those two warblers, but also to a yellow-breasted chat, an ovenbird, and Canada and Connecticut warblers. He had no optical equipment. He didn't even wear glasses, but each bird he identified was confirmed by Huck and Libby with their field guides and binoculars. It was uncanny. The man was back-lighted by the early morning sun, calm, looking upward into the leafy canopy of trees, a cigar butt clinched between his teeth. Then he had an epileptic seizure.

Even as a first year medical student I recognized the condition. I promptly replaced the cigar with a tree branch inserted between his teeth so he wouldn't bite his tongue, and rolled him on his side so he would not aspirate gastric material. Libby raced to a pay phone (no cell phones in 1966) while Huck recited a soothing Buddhist mantra, probably gleaned from his study of East Asian cultures. When the man's convulsion subsided, I checked his coat pockets for identification and found a plastic sandwich bag secured with a red rubber band. Inside were a social security card, a New York Public Library card, and some food stamps. But the name—MacLeish–Archibald MacLeish . . . was this *THE* Archibald MacLeish, poet, playwright, winner of three Pulitzer Prizes, pals with Ernest Hemingway, Ezra Pound, T.S. Elliot? Then the man slowly regained consciousness and explained he had been hit on the head with a rock as a kid in Bayonne, New Jersey, knocked unconscious. He had seizures ever since. The seizures were normally controlled with medication, but for the past few days he'd forgotten to take his pills and had shared some wine last evening in the park with his buddies. Now more alert, he checked his pocket. I sheepishly returned his sandwich bag. "No, I am not *THE* Archibald MacLeish, just a bizarre coincidence. Everyone asks me that. I can't tell a poem from a nursery rhyme. Call me Mac." By then Libby had returned and the paramedics had arrived, but Mac was up on his feet and waved them off. He told us to meet him in the park the next day for more warblers.

And so we did. During the next three years we hunted for shorebirds during fall migration on the beaches of Long Island Sound. We found a rare parliament of snowy owls in winter at Coney Island, kettles of migrating hawks lifted on thermal updrafts along the Palisades—the granite cliffs on the New Jersey side of the Hudson River—and, of course, back in Central Park each spring, the warblers. After some of our outings, Libby invited us to her sumptuous brownstone on Central

Park West, serving hot chocolate in bone china cups and saucers, brandy in Waterford crystal, and scones on a silver platter. During my last year in medical school, Libby, Huck, and I decided to chip in and buy Mac a used pair of 7 x 35 wide-angle Nikon binoculars from a pawn shop for $60. When we gave them to him, he was speechless. Tears eroded furrows between the whiskers of his grimy cheeks. He told us no one before had ever given him a present. He walked off holding his gift as if it were the Hope Diamond.

Two months later I got a phone call from a friend, an intern at St. Luke's Hospital. "Hey, Fisher, don't you have an older, kind of seedy bird-watching buddy with a strange name, Shakespeare, Trollope, or something like that?" "Mac? You mean Archibald MacLeish?" "Yeah, that's it, MacLeish. They've got him down here in the ER. It sounds kind of serious." "I'll be right down." I never took taxis—too expensive. But that night I did. I was in the St. Luke's ER in fifteen minutes. Three policemen were taking notes and talking to witnesses. Behind the draped curtains, now sealed with yellow tape, was Mac's body. Apparently he had been attacked by a gang of punks who had seen his binoculars. He held his precious gift with both hands while a switchblade knife punctured his lungs and then his left kidney. He suffocated while bleeding to death. I called Huck and Libby, but there was nothing we could do. Mac had no known relatives and we had no power of attorney. Fingerprints, photos, and dental impressions were taken, and his body removed to the morgue, where it remained for six weeks and was then cremated. His ashes were strewn in a potter's field behind the old Belleview Hospital without ceremony. We were heartsick. We'd gotten Mac killed over a pair of binoculars he never needed.

After internship, I moved to Arizona. I never saw Libby or Huck again, although we kept in touch with phone calls and Christmas cards. Eventually Libby moved back to Mississippi, where a niece lived nearby to help her. She died five years later at age 86. Huck got his PhD and taught Asian Studies at Berkeley for five years, but then, unexpectedly, died of acute leukemia at age 34. Judy told me the details in a letter. It happened so fast she had no time to call. She still kept the parrot in the antique brass cage.

Now, after all these years, my memory is a bit like a water mirage on a hot asphalt highway in summer—clear at a distance, if perhaps less accurate. It's been forty years since I left New York, but it might have been yesterday. I see Huck loping along on cross-country legs ahead of us to scout; Libby, focusing her exquisite Leitz binoculars with delicate blue fingers; Mac, with his cigar stub and filthy overcoat moving slowly with a slight limp, unerringly spotting birds we would otherwise have missed; and me, tagging along with my borrowed opera glasses. Huck, Libby, Mac, and I were birds of very dissimilar plumage, yet we flocked together, but not by instinct. We chose each other. There is a very special kindness and fellowship among birders, the experienced helping the inexperienced, the young and strong helping the older and frail. Despite a busy medical practice and family responsibilities, I still keep a life list of new bird species. Leafing through my notes, I recall the thrill of my first elegant trogon, rose-throated becard, flame-colored tanager. I also record the names of my companions on each field trip.

I realize now we are all on a migration: the little warblers—the lucky ones that survive storms, collisions with cell phone towers, windmills, and lighted skyscrapers that confuse their star-based navigation; and we humans, the lucky ones surviving illness, divorce, job loss, death of loved ones. We continue on despite life's obstacles. Then, perhaps one day, at an especially dark or lonely moment, we might be suddenly startled by scratchy static overhead. We look upward and are amazed by the energy and courage of a band of little warblers flying northward, casting a shadow for just a brief moment over our shoulder to give us a bit of cheer and let us know it is no longer winter.

# JARVOUS WASHINGTON

In 1907, Harlem Hospital was moved from its original site on the Lower East Side of Manhattan to its present location at 134th Street and Lenox Avenue. It was in this architectural relic that I spent my first month of internship and several clinical rotations during medical school. Of course, there had been some improvements over the years, but certain anachronisms remained.

For example, some of the original unstandardized electrical outlets were still functional. Electricity became widely available in New York in the 1890s, most of it generated by the coal-powered steam turbines at the Pearl Street Station not far from Wall Street. It was not until the 1920s, however, that electrical power was delivered with regulated voltage. Because many of the original outlets at Harlem Hospital were left unsealed with DC current, it was not rare to witness the explosion of an electrocardiogram recorder when an inexperienced medical student or new intern plugged the device into an old outlet that delivered more juice than the sensitive new equipment could handle.

The corridors were dark, illuminated by single oversized incandescent light bulbs spaced approximately thirty feet apart. The only private rooms were designated for infectious cases that required isolation, mostly new cases of tuberculosis that were still contagious. Critical care units were functional, but primitive even by standards of the day. Most patients were treated on open 20—30-bed wards, separate ones for men and women. Beds were lined up in rows like an army barrack. The ancient heavy metal beds themselves, a model of sturdy functionality, were complete with head and foot frames frosted with a white enamel surface. Some of these same beds can now be purchased in exclusive Upper East Side antique stores for more than $1,000.00 each.

That so many patients survived and recovered their health is a tribute to the skills and diligence of the full-time nursing staff and the dedication of the legions of medical students and house staff that trained at Harlem Hospital. The cooperation and camaraderie at the hospital were remarkable. The white interns and residents, mostly from Columbia and Yale; the black house staff, largely from Howard and Meharry; and the nursing staff, nearly all African-American, worked together with devotion and sometimes even joy. At midnight the cafeteria workers prepared a meal for those on call—collard greens, ham hocks, white beans fried in bacon fat, grits, pancakes, and gallons of black coffee. On Fridays we had "liver rounds," when off-duty house staff and nurses would gather for wine tasting, local varietals only: Ripple, Barberpole, Gray Goose, and Peppermint Stick. We'd hang out, chat, and dance to Diana Ross and the Supremes, grooving from a portable record player on top of a file cabinet in the doctors' lounge.

It was into this setting that I admitted Jarvous Washington during my first month of internship, before the old hospital was closed and patients were moved to the new hospital tower. Mr. Washington was a muscular, 6'6", 280-pound piano mover who, to my memory, must have had less than 3% body fat. Undressed, he looked like an illustration from *Gray's Textbook of Anatomy*, demonstrating the origin and insertion of each major muscle. Even the masseter muscles of his jaw rippled with anxiety. Ironically, it was the beverage Ripple, a cheap wine sold in flat glass bottles that fit easily into a jacket pocket, that was largely responsible for Mr. Washington's admission on this and several previous occasions. Jarvous Washington was an alcoholic. It was only when wine money was scarce that he was admitted with alcohol withdrawal, and on this occasion, with its most serious form, delirium tremens (DTs). This condition is a medical emergency. Fluid and electrolyte imbalance can be so severe that kidney failure or heart rhythm disturbances occur not infrequently. Patients with DTs are disorientated, combative, and hallucinatory—like a manic schizophrenic who has just consumed a case of Red Bull, pulled three all-nighters at a job he hates, and then watches as you let the air out of his automobile tires. They are agitated, often unhappy, confused, and out of control in unimaginable ways. Treatment consists of the intravenous replacement of fluids and electrolytes, sedation with intravenous diazepam, and, in those days, the administration of paraldehyde, a viscous solution with a sweet, pungent aroma, given either by nasogastric tube or enema. Intramuscular barbiturates were sometimes given in the emergency department for rapid sedation. Physical restraint was often required until these measures could be instituted.

At 10:00 p.m. the chief medical resident, Jacob Goldberg, told me a patient had been admitted to my service with delirium tremens. The patient had received some sedation in the emergency department and orderlies were now bringing him to the medical ward. I was to call medical records to get his old chart and begin treatment. The patient was Jarvous Washington. On arrival he was mildly sedated, but still quite agitated. He had difficulty answering even simple questions and periodically argued or laughed with a person invisible to me. Goldberg said he would stay with the patient until I returned with the records. I had just spoken with a woman in the medical records department. She was cooperative and actually remembered Mr. Washington from previous admissions. She would have his chart ready for me when I arrived. I spent another five or ten minutes making sure Mr. Washington was stable and IV fluids were running. I recorded notes of his vital signs and physical condition, wrote some preliminary nursing orders, and then walked down the four floors to the medical records department, not trusting the ancient elevators. I rang the bell. There was no answer. The door was normally locked. I opened the unlocked door and called, but there was no answer. I wandered back into the huge stack of ancient filing shelves that, to my imagination, resembled the National Archives.

It was then I found the medial records clerk to whom I had spoken just minutes before, lying on the floor in a pool of blood. At first I thought she was lying face down, but I soon realized that her face and top of her skull no longer existed. Grey gelatinous matter from her frontal cortex and skull fragments blown away at close range by a gunshot defaced the file cabinet labeled Wa–Wh. In her lifeless hand was a large folder—that of Jarvous Washington. I took the blood splattered record, made a quick call to security, and headed back up the stairs, understandably unnerved. The next day her murderer was captured. Identified by security cameras, he was her ex-husband who had just been released from prison.

When I arrived at the medical ward, resident Goldberg was not there, but, more importantly, neither was Jarvous Washington. His empty bed remained, but one of the heavy leather restraints had been torn in half. The other was missing, as was part of the steel bedframe. Blood and intravenous fluid dripped a trail from the ward to the hallway and then down a stairway adjacent to the one I had just ascended. This dark stairwell led to all floors, each connecting to an outdoor fire escape. The stairwell itself was enclosed, dark, and fireproof. A single bare light bulb illuminated the landing at each floor. My next move was decisive but, in retrospect, reckless. I followed the trail of blood and saline down the seldom used dark stairwell with Mr. Washington's chart under my arm. The steps ended in the dark subbasement of Harlem Hospital. The exit door was locked and I came face to face with a large, angry, troubled, disoriented, agitated, piano mover with a disconnected IV line and part of the bed frame and leather restraint dangling from his left wrist. I spoke kindly, gently, if somewhat naïvely: "Mr. Washington, we'd better get back to the medical ward so I can help you get well. You look tired." His response, upon reflection, should have been more predictable, but at the time I was taken aback: "Sheet,youlittlewhitemotherfuckingsoneofabitch. Yo ugokissmyblackasscauseIain'tgonowherewidyou." Or something like that.

Then I remembered Muhammad Ali's first fight with the enormous, menacing, bear-faced ex-convict, Sonny Liston, in 1964. At the prefight physical Ali went nuts. Agitated, yelling, screaming, his pulse rate at 160—it required Angelo Dundee, Bundini Brown, and others to restrain him. Liston was confused, off guard. Was he about to fight a lunatic? Ali was now my guru, my mentor. I worked myself up to a rage. I ripped the cover from Mr. Washington's chart, threw it on the floor, kicked it, spit on the wall, and screamed, "GODDAMIT. Why are we the only ones here to move this fucking Steinway? Dat rich white lady gonna be pissed we don't have her piano by noon. Where are those no good lazy sonofabitch movers? We never gonna get this job done." I had his attention. He was quiet for a moment, and then he spoke, not rationally, but at least with less hostility: "You axe me for help. We do it. Fuck'em. Common l'le fella, you guide de top. Dese damn things not cheap. Steinway, dey play real nice."

Then he began a cadence, a work song that sounded like it might have come from a cotton plantation, a mule train, a southern chain gang. Men working together in unison. The rhythm reminded me of the gospel music that made work and suffering seem bearable. It must have been familiar to piano and furniture movers in the city where many apartments had no elevators and the stairwells were steep and narrow. Mr. Washington began a cadence: "Pick it … Hold it … Go step 1, 2, gimme 2, gimme 2, woah … Haul it, slide it, keep it, move it … I lif' hard, you draw de card, ain't no heaven 'til we get to 7, gimme 2, gimme 2, walk wid de shoe, get to 3, we not free, up to 4, still dere's more, we reach 5, time to jive, 6,7,8 … Fish'in bait, get to 10, den we's men! … Woah … Hold … Gimme 2 …" It was beautiful. Jarvous Washington and I moved that gorgeous, imaginary Steinway grand piano all the way up five floors to the medical ward—all the way up to that beautiful Fifth Avenue penthouse where that imaginary rich old white lady was waiting for us. We did it without any help, just the two of us.

When we got back to the medical ward, Mr. Washington told me, "That a lot of work, lil fella. I rest now." And he did. Maybe the drugs were finally kicking in. I secured a new IV line, administered more fluids with potassium and magnesium, more diazepam, and placed some new leather arm and leg restraints, just in case. Then, as I was finishing my physical examination, completing the nursing orders and paperwork, resident Goldberg was back. "Aren't you done yet, Fisher? Geeez. You've got another admission in the ER. Sounds like a woman in septic shock."

I survived internship, but doctors were being drafted for the war in Vietnam. Physicians could also satisfy their military obligation by serving in the United States Public Health Service (USPHS). I had always been interested in Native Americans and was fortunate to be assigned to the USPHS Indian Hospital in Winslow, Arizona, near the Navajo and Hopi Reservations. Before I left New York, I took one last bus ride up Amsterdam Avenue from Harlem Hospital to the Columbia–Presbyterian Medical Center. By chance, I saw a large moving van parked by the curb at 138th Street: "Washington Brothers, Piano and Furniture Movers." I couldn't remember if Jarvous had brothers. I hoped he was okay. I packed and left New York the next day. My father gave me a used 1968 four-wheel-drive Ford Bronco. It took me two weeks to make the trip from New York to Arizona. There was no need to hurry.

# HOSTEEN BISCHITTY

After an adventuresome two-week drive on the backroads of America, I arrived in Arizona and entered a different world. A short drive north from the town of Winslow was the absolute stillness of the Little Painted Desert. There was no noise from taxis, subways, police sirens, hot dog vendors, or buses. I was aware of a strange ticking sound until I realized that it was coming from my Timex watch. The desert was that quiet. As I scanned the landscape I could visualize the vast Paleolithic sea that once covered this area, alive with fang-toothed fish and plesiosaurs hunting the tropical waters, now dry and bare, the strata of multicolored sandstone, and an occasional fossil, the only evidence of this ancient ocean and its creatures.

The next day I met the other doctors. We got acquainted and made rounds at the hospital. I was assigned to work three days a week at Dilkon, a clinic thirty-three miles northeast of Winslow. Accompanying me in a four-wheel-drive International Harvester truck were Vera Dillon, a public health nurse, and Cecil Clinton, our driver. Both Vera and Cecil were full-blooded Navajo and members of the Slow Talking Clan. They knew all the families in the area and, of course, spoke fluent Navajo. In fact, Cecil had been a code talker during the Second World War, a member of the elite group of Navajo Indians who spoke to each other in a Navajo code that was never deciphered by the Japanese. Cecil was responsible for saving many lives during the war.

Our first stop was usually at the hogan of Hosteen Bischitty, a dignified man in his early 70s. Bischitty was an Hitali, a medicine man. He dressed in the traditional manner, his long gray hair gathered in a bun tied with a white cord. He usually wore a green velveteen shirt with silver buttons, a turquoise necklace, turquoise earrings, and silver bracelets on both wrists. Bischitty also had active tuberculosis. He lived in the hogan with his wife and four grandchildren, who had all had become infected with tuberculosis from Hosteen. He was cautious and reluctant to accept white man's medicine. When I showed him his chest x-ray, he was impressed and told me the radiographic abnormalities were caused by smoke that would blow away. He would only take medicine with supervision and not without a "needle piercing." Many Navajos were fascinated by medicine that was injected into the tissues. As a result, we visited his hogan three times a week to be sure he swallowed the pills—rifampin, ethambutol, and isoniazid—and administered the "needle-piercing," intramuscular streptomycin. He appreciated the Bellagonna (white man's) way of injecting spirits through a needle into the body, but he never accepted or understood our methods. Why did we ask so many questions? ("Where does it hurt? How long have you had the cough?") A real healer should know these things. In the Navajo way, a hand trembler would locate the illness, an herbalist would provide a remedy, and, for more serious conditions, a hitali, a medicine man, like Bischitty, would perform a ceremonial sing. Except for the "piercing of skin with spirit," the young white doctors, in Bischitty's opinion, had a lot to learn.

The name "Hosteen Bischitty" means, "man with automobile," in Navajo. Hosteen owned a Ford Model T which had long ago collapsed on the rough reservation roads. His nephew, a motorpool mechanic in the US Army during the Korean conflict, was supposedly an expert in auto repair. Because of Hosteen's early automobile ownership and the undeserved reputation of his nephew as an expert mechanic, many people brought their trucks to be repaired at Bischitty's place. Quite obviously, neither of the two men knew the first thing about auto repair or maintenance. The area around the hogan resembled a junkyard, littered with the rusting bodies of at least twenty or thirty cars and trucks. It was into this wreckage that Hosteen released three very aggressive goats. In order to reach Hosteen and administer the medication, Vera, Cecil, and I had to run a gauntlet through the rusting chassis of the trucks and cars to avoid the hostile goats lurking among the ruined vehicles, waiting to attack. Hosteen thought this was all great fun. We devised a strategy. Cecil and I would decoy the goats while Vera headed for the hogan with the medication and injections. Over the two years that I was in Winslow, this adventure was repeated three times a week. At the end of two years, Hosteen and his family were cured.

Vera and Cecil were great storytellers. It was during one of the drives back and forth to Dilkon that Vera said to me, "Dr. Jeff, did I ever tell you the story about Tom Finney? You remind me of him." I told her I'd never heard the story. She changed the names because the Navajo are not allowed to speak the names of the dead. This is the story that Vera told me,

*Tom Finney and his wife, Sara, also a physician, had been assigned to the Winslow Hospital about five years before my arrival. They were good doctors and had outgoing, engaging personalities. They were well-liked and respected by the Navajo and Hopi patients. Tom and Sara immersed themselves in Indian culture and spent weekends hunting for petroglyphs, exploring ruins, and attending Navajo, Hopi, and Zuni ceremonials and powwows. One weekend they decided to search for an isolated ruin they'd read about in the magazine,* Arizona Highways. *They drove from Winslow to Flagstaff and then north to Tuba*

*City and Kayenta along old Route 89 to the Shonto Plateau. It was in January, the Navajo season "when thunder sleeps." By the time they reached their destination, it was already getting dark and snow clouds loomed low in the sky. They passed the Cow Springs Trading Post, then drove half a mile to where directions led them north on a dirt road marked by three juniper trees and a cattle guard. They followed this road for 2.8 miles until it forked. They took the right fork, as directed. By this time it had gotten quite dark and a heavy, wet snow began to fall. Sara urged Tom to return to the Thunderbird Motel in Kayenta to spend the night. They could return the next day to explore the ruin. Tom felt they were almost at the destination and wanted to continue. He drove a bit further down the road. Now the snowstorm was in full force, their headlights magnifying the heavy flakes blowing toward the windshield. Beyond their headlights was absolute darkness. There were no stars, no moon, no lights.*

*Then, in the far distance, they saw the figure of a man appear, walking toward them along the edge of the road illuminated by their headlights. He was dressed in the uniform of the U.S. Army. As he approached their vehicle they could see his nameplate pinned over the left pocket of his olive green uniform: "Chischilly." They also noticed a deep scar along his left cheek. He motioned for them to roll down the window. Then he spoke to them in English with a Navajo accent. "This is not your way. Ahead there is a cliff that falls 1,000 feet into the canyon below. You will not see it. There is no warning. Turn around and go back. This is not your time to die." The Finneys asked where he came from. "I come from a different place. Your way is not my way, but later we will all take the same path." They were puzzled by these words, but decided to turn around, follow the man's instructions, and drive back to Kayenta to spend the night. In the short time it took them to make a U-turn through the sagebrush, the man disappeared into the night.*

*The next day the Finneys returned by the same route, past the Cow Springs Trading Post, and down the road they had followed the night before. The sky was now a clear blue. The snow had stopped falling and there had been no wind so they could easily follow their tracks. They took the right fork, but for the first time they noticed a hogan off to the side of the road. An old woman was chopping wood. They called out, "Ya'at'eeh Shimasani" (Hello, Grandmother). The old woman hurried inside. A few minutes later a teenage girl dressed in a Western shirt, Wrangler blue jeans, and roughout boots approached their truck. She asked if they needed help. The Finney's told her they'd been there last night, looking for the Cow Springs Ruins. They'd talked to a man in an Army uniform who seemed to appear from nowhere and then vanished. His name was Chischilly. Did she know anything about this man?*

*Abruptly, the girl took a few steps back from the truck. The color seemed to drain from her face. Her eyes scanned the horizon and she became frightened. "What you say is not possible. There is no one here by that name. My uncle, Ben Chischilly, was killed in Vietnam a year ago." Tom asked if he had any distinctive markings or scars. The girl said that he had a long scar on his cheek from a rodeo accident. The Finneys looked at each other. Then the girl said to them, rather nervously, "Agoneh" (I'm leaving now) and ran back inside her hogan. Tom and Sara followed their tire tracks in the snow. They saw where they had stopped and turned around the night before. They parked the truck and walked for about a quarter of a mile down the road. Just as they were told by the mysterious soldier the night before, the road ended abruptly and without warning. Ahead were a rocky precipice, the ancient Anasszi ruin, and a canyon floor a thousand feet below. They looked carefully in the snow and saw the footprints of an Army issue shoe paralleling the road, but as the footprints got closer to the edge of the cliff they became the tracks of a coyote. The Finneys became frightened and decided to return to Winslow. Vera told them the tracks in the snow were probably those of a Chindi—a human spirit that had taken the form of an animal. The Chindi have power to harm or help human beings.*

*The following year, Tom and Sara were skiing in Durango, Colorado. On the drive back they glimpsed a coyote, crossing the road directly in front of them. Tom instinctively hit the brakes on a patch of black ice. The car spun out of control and hit the cement embankment of a bridge. Sara was killed instantly. Tom broke his pelvis, both legs, his left shoulder and sustained a severe head injury. He was stabilized in Durango and then flown to the intensive care unit at the University of Colorado. It was ten days before he regained consciousness and weeks before the doctors told him about Sara. Guilt and sorrow sent Dr. Tom Finney into a deep depression.*

*Months after he had recovered from his physical injuries, Tom returned to Winslow but was unable to work because of severe depression. He was given a medical furlough to Phoenix, where he was hospitalized and received intensive psychotherapy, anti-depressants, and ultimately, electroconvulsive therapy, but to no benefit. He was preparing to receive a medical discharge and return to his family in Ohio when Vera made a suggestion: "Dr. Tom, perhaps Hosteen Bischitty could help you." Bischitty was a respected medicine man, an "hitali," who possessed detailed knowledge of many ceremonial sings. He could perform the Blessingway for Dr. Finney, a three-day ceremony designed to purify a person's spirit from disharmony. Tom had nothing to lose. For three days the doctor subjected himself to hours in the sweat lodge and night-long chants. He was blessed with corn pollen. His body was surrounded by sand paintings intricately detailed by members of Hosteen's clan, and he was blessed in the traditional manner.*

*After the ceremony, there was no visible change. Dr. Tom Finney was still in a deep depression. But after a week or two he began to regain his appetite. Then his smile and sense of humor gradually returned. After six weeks he was almost back to normal. He finished his final year of service in Winslow and returned to Ohio State University for a residency in orthopedic surgery. After completing his training, he accepted a position at a hospital in Farmington, New Mexico, where he met a Navajo pediatrician. They were married two years later in a traditional Navajo ceremony in Canyon De Chelly.*

After Vera told me this story, I asked her more about the Blessingway. She said she really didn't know much about the ceremony. It was complicated and long, but she knew the words at the end: "Walk in beauty. Beauty goes before you and follows you. Beauty walks beside you. Beauty is above you and below you. You are surrounded by beauty. You walk in beauty. You have become beauty."

For the Navajo, physical and mental illness result from loss of harmony (Hozo). A ceremonial sing like the Blessingway restores harmony, and hence, health. The "smoke" cleaned from Hosteen's lungs and from Dr. Finney's mind by the willingness of these two men to accept a form of treatment alien to their culture. Afterward, both Hosteen Bischitty and Dr. Finney could walk again in beauty, in good health, in harmony.

# THE WOMAN WITH NO NAME

Autumn is the season the Navajo call "the time of slender wind." Cecil Clinton, our driver, Vera Dillon, the public health nurse, and I drove the International Harvester four-wheel drive truck past Hosteen Bischitty's hogan. We had visited him the previous day on the way to the Dilkon Clinic thirty-three miles northeast of Winslow, Arizona, on historic Route 66. We were driving through a torrential downpour so violent the windshield wipers could barely keep up with the rain. A cold snap had arrived, and snow was predicted. The dirt roads were rivers of red mud. Cecil shifted into four-wheel drive. Due to the weather, it would probably be a light day at the clinic. We were in good spirits.

Cecil mentioned that his friend, Sam Todachinie, had purchased a small horse in Albuquerque a few days ago. I asked, "Was it an eohippus?" Cecil and Vera looked puzzled. Then, in unison, they asked, "What's an eohippus, Dr. Fisher?" I explained that eohippus was the first horse living in North America approximately forty million years ago after the extinction of the dinosaurs. Eohippus was about three feet tall and weighed nearly sixty pounds. I was joking. Both Cecil and Vera broke out in laughter at the idea of a three-foot tall horse with such an odd name. The Navajo have a keen sense of humor, especially with wordplay. Things were quiet for a few moments; then Vera would whisper from the back seat, "eohippus." Hysterical laughter would consume us again.

As we had anticipated, it was a slow day at the clinic. There were a few prenatal visits, well-baby checks, a fresh arm laceration from a chainsaw mishap that needed suturing, a few head colds, and a lady with a urinary tract infection that the Navajo call "ant sickness." Finally, at the end of the day, as we were packing up to head back to Winslow, the woman entered the clinic. Things changed. The staff grew quiet and, though normally helpful, stepped away from the woman. Jeanette Peaches, the LPN, got a string of ghost beads from her purse and hung them around her neck. Ghost bead necklaces are made from Juniper nutshells after insects have eaten the substance inside. A small hole is punctured at each end of the shell, then strung on a light cord and tied to make a necklace. They are attractive and are often sold at Indian powwows. They are also believed to protect the wearer from evil spirits.

The woman appeared to be in her sixties and was wrapped in a multicolored wool Pendleton blanket draped over her shoulders, now soaked with the heavy rain. She wore a traditional green velveteen dress and was adorned with turquoise and silver jewelry. She moved slowly and deliberately, making no eye contact but pointed her chin in the direction she wished to take, a familiar Navajo gesture. She climbed onto the exam table without help and waited. There was

THE WOMAN WITH NO NAME

no medical record, but some of our staff knew her, or at least knew of her reputation. She was from Ganado, a part of the vast Navajo reservation far to the east. She had never been to Dilkon before. Then she looked tangentially in my direction and put her left hand over her ear. I approached her like any other patient, looked into her left ear canal with an otoscope, and saw a red, slightly bulging eardrum. She had a low-grade fever but no regional lymphadenopathy.

The rest of her examination was normal. She had acute otitis media, easily treated with a course of antibiotics, but is less common in adults than in children. Jeanette said a few words to her in Navajo. She nodded her head but did not speak. I decided to give her an intramuscular injection of Rocephin. She didn't speak English and could be unreliable to take oral medication for ten days. Also, she may have been allergic to penicillin. Vera told her the doctor would pierce her body with a powerful liquid. She was told to see an Indian Health Service doctor when she returned to Ganado. Adults with acute otitis media may have other issues, like nasopharyngeal carcinoma, but she was only told to seek follow up. She agreed.

Jeanette and Vera asked me how I felt. I was unsure about the nature of their question. The woman appeared to be in her sixties with an ear infection. She smelled of wet wool, wood smoke, and a lack of bathing. They persisted, "Was there anything else you noticed? Are you OK, Dr. Fisher?" I was unsure where this conversation was going, but also sensed that this was not the time or place to ask more questions.

On the ride back to Winslow there was no laughter about eohippus. I asked what had happened at the clinic, but Vera and Cecil were reluctant to talk further. They both looked concerned. Vera tried to change the subject: "Are you going skiing this winter, Dr. Fisher?" After a long pause, Cecil finally revealed that the woman had never been to the Dilkon area before. She was known to have a special ability to see things that others could not. She was not evil, but knowledge of her unexplained clairvoyance put our clinic staff on guard. They did not speak her name. Navajo lore teaches that to speak the names of the deceased or supernatural beings could cause trouble. Many Navajos are very superstitious and, for example, will go to great lengths to hide hair and fingernail clippings lest they fall into the hands of an evil spirit, like a chindi or a skinwalker who could use them to cast evil against the person.

The woman was asked by the Yazzie family to come to Dilkon to help them. Emma and Ben Yazzie had two children, ages twelve and eight, who had gone missing. They were herding the family's sheep and had not returned by nightfall. Local search parties and the Navajo Tribal Police were called but could not locate them. Emma had a sister in Ganado who knew the woman and asked if she could come to help. Emma would pay. Cecil told me later that when the woman arrived, she entered the Yazzie hogan and sat inside facing the east wall. She went into a trance-like state, singing softly to herself words that were inaudible to others. After two hours, the woman stood up and approached the Yazzies with tears in her eyes.

The Navajo, like other Native Americans, do not have well-defined descriptive terms for distance or for short periods of time. For this reason, the woman had a different way of recounting her vision: "At sunrise (about 7 a.m.) walk in the direction where the sun sleeps (west) until the sun greets the hair (10 a.m., about three hours). You will see two piñon trees twisted around each other with a manzanita bush surrounding them. Turn to face the Sacred Mountains in Flagstaff and walk until the sun climbs overhead (noon, about two hours). You will find a shallow ravine or arroyo. Walk into this arroyo and follow it until the sun goes behind the Sacred Mountains. There you will see six large stones forming the pattern of flying geese. Turn towards to the Hopi Mesas and walk slowly one thousand paces to a large grove of piñon trees. Under the trees are the boy and his sister. They have frozen to death. The sheep are nearby." The woman was paid and returned home. The Tribal Police followed her instructions and found the children the next day. Light snow began to fall. The woman had experienced similar visions many times before.

When I left New York for Arizona, I was prepared for things to be different on the Navajo reservation. A friend gave me a book, *Navajo Witchcraft*, by Clyde Kluckhohn, a Harvard trained anthropologist. Kluckhohn spent many years among the Navajo, and learned to speak their difficult language fluently. His book, now a classic, a scholarly nonfiction treatise but, for me, still just a book. Later, during my years in Winslow, I discovered the engaging and bestselling detective stories by Tony Hillerman, recounting crimes solved with a combination of good police work and knowledge of Navajo traditions and lore. These were engaging stories about places on the reservation I had visited, stories of fiction. At the Dilkon Clinic that day, I experienced the surreal first hand, not from a book. I could not detect anything unusual about the woman: no aura, no vibes, no goosebumps. The hair on my neck did not stand up.

Assuredly, there were aspects of her presence beyond my understanding, detected by our Native American staff. I reflected on the Hillerman novels and the studies by Kluckhohn. These writings conveyed certain truths about the Navajo and their land, which I was previously prepared to dismiss, or at least not to take seriously. Nonetheless, I can say with certainty, on that cold, rainy day, in "the time of slender wind," I was in the presence of unknown forces and was required to suspend my previous way of thinking. Also, my traditional Navajo companions, adhering to Navajo lore, would not speak the name of the woman who could see beyond this realm. Doing so could bring trouble just as if they spoke the names of deceased friends or family. There are certain things that should not be done.

# POLINGAYSI QOYAWAYMA

An elderly Hopi woman was "standing on a corner in Winslow, Arizona," in 1972, the same summer the Eagles released their hit song, "Take it Easy." Without warning, the woman was suddenly struck off the sidewalk by a drunk driver in a flatbed Ford pickup truck and brought to the Winslow Indian Hospital by an ambulance. She was indeed, as the Eagles sang, "a sight to see."

I recalled the woman and the circumstances of her accident when I visited Winslow after a 36-year absence. Time has not been kind to Winslow, or other small towns along historic Route 66, that ribbon of asphalt and concrete that connects the pier in Santa Monica, California, to downtown Chicago. When I left Winslow in 1972, the highway divided as it entered town, two one-way streets, both lined with stores, attracting tourists and local residents: Yellow Front, where I bought fishing hooks and bait; Western Auto, for fan belts and motor oil; the Prairie Moon Café, where Sidney Poolheco's country-western band played on Fridays and Saturdays; Lorenzo Hubbell's Trading

Post, stacked with Navajo rugs, Hopi pottery, and Native American jewelry; and Wayne Troutner's Store for Men, which lured fathers, husbands, and lonely truckers into town with large billboards every four or five miles along Route 66 depicting a buxom and scantily clad cowgirl in red leather boots: "Troutner's, just for men." Troutner sold Western clothing for men: hats, boots, vests, shirts ... nothing more.

When the Highway Department decided travelers wanted speed and efficiency, not charm and local variety, they built Interstate 40 and bypassed Winslow entirely. On October 9, 1979, I-40 opened and the lifeblood was slowly drained from Winslow and other small towns across America, our travel adventures now mongrels of sameness.

There were, however, some pleasant memories that awaited me on that return visit. The sweet smell of juniper smoke burning from many fireplaces still gives the night air a distinctive and pleasing aroma. KINO Radio continues to broadcast the livestock reports in the Navajo language and gives the names of those individuals arrested for public drunkenness, using the euphemism "drinking from an open container." I never could get the hang of drinking from a closed container. There were also two very special surprises. The spectacular Fred Harvey Lodge, La Posada, built in 1930 and once used as the business offices for the Santa Fe Railroad, was rescued from demolition by a coalition of historical preservation groups and restored to its original splendor in this dying town by a private investor, at a cost of twelve million dollars. Another pleasant surprise was the new Northland Pioneer College located just 200 yards from the house I rented in 1970. It was the name on the college's main building that stopped me: The Blunk Health Science Center, named for Burley and Josephine Blunk. During a 33-year nursing career, first in the Army and then with the

Indian Health Service, Josephine Blunk, RN, had seen almost every emergency, far more than the young and inexperienced doctors who served at the Winslow Indian Hospital.

The injured Hopi woman, now in our ER, had a fractured humerus and clavicle, multiple broken ribs that had punctured and collapsed her right lung, the thoracic cavity now filling with blood and air. She also had a compound, displaced fracture of her right femur. Despite these injuries, she was remarkably alert and calm, though her breathing was becoming more labored and her blood pressure dropping. She appeared to be in her late 70s and wore her graying hair with traditional Hopi straight bangs across her forehead. A necklace of rounded heshi beads made from shell and turquoise complemented her crisp blue cotton jacket and skirt now drenched with blood, which we removed to allow inspection of her injuries. Her posture was hunched forward, in all likelihood from osteoporosis, giving her a faint resemblance to the humpbacked flute player, Kokopelli, a mythical figure from the ancient Anasszi people who inhabited the Southwest centuries ago.

Nurse Blunk directed us in such a way that we believed we were the ones in charge: "Would you doctors like me to start a subclavian line? Our patient looks like she's drying up and may need some juice and a few gallons of blood. Dr. Fisher, why don't you grab her leg and give it a gentle tug. Turn the ankle inward while I give her a shot of morphine and some lidocaine into the hematoma. That jagged bone looks like it's making the femoral artery nervous. It's making me nervous too. Doctor, have you ever put in a chest tube? Well, of course you have, dear. It would be easier though if we had a chest tube. Well, see those scissors? Let's cut up a big Foley catheter and stick it through her ribs with this hemostat. Remember, walk it over the rib, not under.

We don't want any more bleeding, do we? There, I've finished the IV, love. Let me get you some bandages. I'll crank up the Gomco suction so we can get our patient breathing. Hand me that oxygen mask will you, honey? You doctors are doing real fine, just fine."

Under Nurse Blunk's expert supervision, Bill Mings, Larry Wallach, and I had stabilized our patient. The makeshift chest tube draining the hemopneumothorax reexpanded her lung. She was typed and cross-matched for three units of packed red blood cells, which we then administered while Nurse Blunk ordered a helicopter to fly her to a large referral center in Gallop, New Mexico, to be managed in the intensive care unit by a surgical team. We talked to an orthopedic surgeon on the telephone before her departure and he was surprised to learn that we had done so well with the complexity of her injuries. But then he had never met Josaphine Blunk, RN. I accompanied the patient on the flight to Gallop with a Hopi nurse, Ruth Yoyoyetewa.

During her ordeal in the Winslow ER, our patient's manner seemed unusually placid given the circumstances. I even got the impression that she was not especially worried whether she lived or died. She seemed resigned to her fate, although she was not fatalistic—quite the opposite. She joked with us about our makeshift chest tube: "At least you didn't have to use an enema tube. I hope you doctors remember which tube goes where when you remove them." This got all of us laughing. She remarked how fast we removed her blouse and skirt: "Now that's what I call experience." Our patient termed the helicopter flight "an adventure." She had never flown before. When we dropped her off at the Gallup Indian Medical Center she promised she would return to Winslow before long and said she would be on her best behavior with all of the men and bars in Gallup.

On the return flight to Winslow, Ruth, the nurse who accompanied me on the flight, told me our patient was quite famous. Her name was Polingaysi Qoyawayma, which in the Hopi language means "butterfly sitting among the flowers in the breeze." She was a childhood friend of Ruth's mother. Polingaysi was also known by her married name, Elizabeth White, from a brief, unsuccessful marriage. Polingaysi Qoyawayma was born in the town of Oraibi on the Hopi Reservation. Oraibi is the oldest continually occupied site in North America, with artifacts dating the location to at least 1050 AD Polingaysi loved her home on the Hopi mesas and the traditions of her people. Long before her conversion to Christianity by Mennonite missionaries, she would sit on the edge of the mesa with her father and offer prayers to the morning sun. But she was an independent and restless spirit. She wanted more from life than that of that of a Hopi wife—cooking meals, carrying water and firewood, and living in a pueblo with mud floors.

Ruth told me when Polingaysi returned to Oraibi after four years of study at the Sherman Indian School in Riverside, California, her people no longer considered her one of them. She had become a "bahana," a white woman. Oddly, she was considered "colored" by Anglo people and was not allowed to eat in restaurants or sit in trains or buses with whites. Polingaysi decided to become an elementary school teacher. Unlike the methods used at Sherman where the customs and language of Native American people were condemned, Polingaysi encouraged native children to use their own language. She gradually taught them English, mathematics, and other subjects by incorporating aspects from their own traditions and language with which they were familiar. After a 31-year teaching career, mostly on the Hopi Reservation, she was awarded a medal for excellence in teaching and leadership among Indian people by John Collier, Secretary of the Department of Interior. Nonetheless, Polingaysi still felt something was missing from her life. She loved her years of teaching, but felt unfulfilled.

When she was in her late sixties, a violent sandstorm struck the Hopi mesas. When the storm subsided, she opened her eyes and noticed that the grains of sand were a mixture of colors: white, brown, red, and black, all mixed together like the people of the world. She then had an inspiration that would lead her in a new direction. Polingaysi would mold and use the sand to fashion clay and then form pottery with her own artistic innovations, breaking from the traditional patterns and colors of Hopi pottery. Today, her distinctive pottery is exhibited next to those of other famous pueblo potters, Fanny Nampeyo, Margaret Tafoya, and Maria Martinez. Polingaysi's works are on display at the Heard Museum in Phoenix, AZ, the Smithsonian Institution in Washington, D.C., and in many other museums and private collections around the world.

Four weeks after the accident, Polingaysi returned from Gallup to Winslow and completed rehabilitation. We attempted to remove the cast from her leg, but our cast cutter broke and the remaining plaster had to be pried apart with a beer can opener and a screw driver. Still, with her sense of humor, she remarked, "Now I know how you doctors spend your time." She looked at the can opener. "Where's the beer? Where's my party? No, I'm just kidding. Don't be shocked, Dr. Fisher." Weeks later she arranged for me to attend a Kiva ceremony in the village of Mishongnovi at Second Mesa. The nurse who had flown with me to Gallup, Ruth Yoyoyetewa, would meet me there. Polingaysi knew that I was interested in Indian culture and wanted me to have direct experience with the sacred ceremonial life of her Hopi people.

Early in the evening, I crossed the ice-covered bridge over the Little Colorado River, passed the turn-off to Dilkon and Seba Dalki, and continued north on State Route 87. I noticed a dust devil, a mini swirling tornado, off to the side of the road. It seemed prophetic. This is a sign to the Hopi people that the voices of their ancestors are speaking, carried to earth in the swirling vortex. To the west rose the snow-capped peaks of the San Francisco mountains, home of the Katsina spirits. To the east stood the twin smokestacks of the Cholla Power Plant, their industrial forms a blasphemy, mimicking the slender bodies of the two Sacred Corn Maidens. When I arrived at Mishongnovi on Second Mesa, the sun had set and darkness surrounded the village. There was no moon, and clouds obscured the stars. It was cold, and a wind picked up from the north. I parked on the edge of the village as directed and walked to the Kiva, where Ruth would meet me. I was told to climb onto the roof, but Ruth was nowhere in sight. Suddenly I was surrounded by ten or twelve enormous men dressed in full Katsina regalia—wolves, ogres, mud-heads, and other masked figures, grunting and making deep throated sounds from inside their masks. I was frightened. Had I done everything right? A white man, I was alone in the darkness on the roof of a sacred Kiva. Then, one of the men dressed as a wolf Katsina, without speaking, took my arm and led me to the ladder. He motioned for me to descend into the Kiva. I climbed carefully down the ladder into the ceremonial chamber where I saw Ruth sitting on a bench on the opposite side. She nodded and smiled. I sat with about twenty or thirty other Hopi people who were quiet and respectful. After approximately thirty minutes, the first group of Katsina dancers descended the ladder and began to perform. The sounds of their chanting music reflected from the adobe walls of this tiny chamber. It was magical and breathtaking, a perfect rhythm building and then subsiding in unison from the dancers, their chants muffled inside heavy masks, the singing punctuated by gourd hand rattles and tortoise shell rattles filled with pebbles and strapped to their legs, keeping time with the rhythm. Their torsos were bare. Hopi sashes dangled from their waists. Each dance lasted twenty to thirty minutes and then there was silence. The dancers exited into the night sky by the same ladder they had descended. All remained silent until another group of dancers descended the ladder. During the course of the night, there were eight or ten separate dances.

The ceremony finally ended about six in the morning when a glint of sunlight illuminated the eastern sky. I'd been in the Kiva for six hours. I thanked Ruth and some of the others and then wearily drove back to Winslow, where I slept the rest of the morning and early afternoon. That evening I reflected on the familiarity of my little rented house on a quiet street in White America where kids rode their skateboards home from school, fathers mowed the grass, and mothers returned home from grocery shopping in station wagons. On the Reservation, just two hours away, life was very different. Kids help plant corn, mothers make blue piki bread, and fathers dress for ceremonies in masks and animal skins.

Polingaysi could have written the lyrics for the Eagles: "We may lose or we may win, though we will never be here again, so take it easy, take it easy." She was a remarkable and dignified woman, who like Josephine Blunk, was gifted with a wonderful sense of humor that helped her bridge two very different cultures. She died in 1990, after 98 winters.

# Troy Bylas

After a two-year residency in internal medicine at the University of New Mexico, I returned to the Indian Health Service and joined the staff of the Phoenix Indian Medical Center (PIMC) as one of four internists. At ten o'clock one morning, I received a call from Dr. John Saari, a new physician at the San Carlos Indian Hospital. He sounded worried. He had a 16-year-old Apache youth in the emergency room with a two-week history of joint pain, fever, and shortness of breath. He appeared desperately ill. Dr. Saari found prominent lymph nodes, an enlarged spleen, rapid pulse, and a temperature of 101°. I told him to call a helicopter and fly the patient to Phoenix, where I would assume his care. I identified with the stresses facing Dr. Saari and other young doctors working alone in remote areas, accepting the responsibility for the care of seriously ill or critically injured patients, as I had done for two years in Winslow close to the Navajo Reservation.

Two hours later, the young man, accompanied by his mother, arrived by helicopter on the landing pad of the Phoenix Indian Medical Center. Troy Bylas was a tall, wiry teenager in Wrangler blue jeans, a threadbare Phoenix Suns T-shirt, and shoulder-length black hair. He was very sick indeed. I confirmed the presence of enlarged lymph nodes, hepatosplenomegaly, and petechiae (small hemorrhages in the skin) over his legs and lower abdomen. But what I remember most were his eyes. They were not hostile or frightened, but calm, wise, and courageous, similar to the eyes of the Apache Chief Geronimo, the young Geronimo, "Goy-An-Thlay" (the one who yawns), before Mexican troops killed his wife and children.

We needed to take samples of blood, spinal fluid, and bone marrow. I requested permission from his mother, Susan Bylas, who was the head of the medical records department at San Carlos and familiar with "white man's medicine." The father, an Apache medicine man himself, was hostile. He had driven his truck from San Carlos to Phoenix, not trusting helicopters or white doctors. He made no eye contact and pretended to speak only Apache, although I knew he spoke English from talking with Dr. Saari. Troy's mother had already given permission for treatment. His father wanted to check him out of the hospital to perform a traditional Apache healing ceremony. Fortunately, the Apache tribe is matriarchal. The mother is the trunk of the tree, the children are the branches, the father, or husband, are the leaves, dropping off in season (to go fishing, hunting, or drinking), while the trunk and branches remain. With his mother's permission we performed the necessary tests that confirmed our suspected diagnosis of acute lymphocytic leukemia. A hematologist from St. Joseph's Hospital was consulted and chemotherapy begun. Treatments consisted of the intravenous infusion of prednisolone, vincristine, and daunorubicin, as well as intrathecal (injections into the spinal fluid itself) with prednisolone and methotrexate. While giving these treatments, Troy and I discussed the chances of the Phoenix Suns making the playoffs and his prospects on the Globe High School team. He was delighted I had a subscription to *Sports Illustrated* and brought the most recent issues to his room. After just three weeks the change was miraculous. Troy was skateboarding around the vinyl floors of the Indian Medical Center. He needed to be discharged not so much for his own good, but for the welfare of the floor nurses who served as Troy's slalom posts as they attempted to deliver medication to other patients on the medical floor. I cautioned him to take it easy. He'd wink.

Troy returned to San Carlos under the supervision of Dr. Saari. I kept track of him by phone and with monthly visits to the hospital. Things seemed to be going well. Troy was now a junior at Globe High School and was the starting point guard on the basketball team. One night, Susan invited Dr. Saari and me for dinner and then to watch Troy play in a game against Globe's arch rival, Miami. We drove to town in the Bylases' white Ford pickup to a crowded gymnasium, exploding with the yells of teenagers and parents of the players. It was beautiful to watch Troy lead his team up and down the court. The long, shiny black hair that had come out in bunches during chemotherapy had now regrown, thick, shiny, and shoulder length. With the grace and agility of an Apache warrior he did crossover dribbles with the ease of Michael Jordan, he saw the whole court without turning his head, hitting the open man cutting to the basket with a no-look, behind-the-back pass. He scored 28 points, had 14 assists, 10 rebounds, and 4 steals. The Globe Tigers crushed the Miami Vandals 72 to 50. After the game Troy looked up to the stands where we were sitting and flashed the victory sign.

On other visits to the clinic Susan would often invite me to lunch. Mr. Bylas always seemed to have something to do and would leave, without a word, as soon as I arrived. One afternoon, while having lunch in the Bylases' kitchen, I looked through the window and saw a peculiar fluttering in the backyard bushes. I went out to check. A hummingbird had been captured by a praying mantis camouflaged in a Lantana bush! The little bird's struggles were over, its broken wings firmly clasped in the insect's spiked forelegs. It seemed so unreal, so unexpected, so unjust.

Fourteen months after our initial conversation, Dr. Saari called from San Carlos. Troy's fever had returned. He was weak and pale. The family drove him to Phoenix, where my fears were confirmed: the leukemia had returned. A new round of chemotherapy was administered, but this time the course was less favorable. Troy was given oxygen, transfusions, and intravenous chemotherapy, but nothing seemed to help. He lost weight and his long black hair. The bone marrow was packed with leukemic cells, displacing the healthy ones. Susan asked me if the hospital would permit her husband and other medicine men to perform a ceremony at Troy's bedside. It was not unusual for traditional healing ceremonies to be done by various tribal groups at the Indian Medical Center. Mr. Bylas and three drummers arrived. For the next five days at sundown, sacred corn pollen was dusted on Troy's body. Drums, rattles, and chants blessed Troy and others down the corridor of the medical ward. It reminded me of the rich gospel music I heard years before at Harlem Hospital, the music and rhythms restoring a sense of peace and harmony. The faint sweet aroma of piñon smoke drifted from Troy's room.

Despite everything, Troy's health continued to deteriorate. One evening, before going home, I stopped by his room. Mr. Bylas was sitting at Troy's bedside with the drummers. It was the first time he spoke to me. "You are a good doctor. You are a good man, but white man's medicine is not strong enough. Apache medicine cannot help my boy. He is like a bird with broken wings. Soon he will see the Holy Ones." Then he reached into his pocket and handed me a small package. "I made this for you." He gave me a silver nameplate inlaid with turquoise: "J. Fisher, M.D." Thanking him would take away his kindness according to Apache tradition. I wore that nameplate until I retired. Then he gave me the limp handshake characteristic of North American Indians, who are not familiar with this tradition among white people. Troy appeared to be sleeping, but when I touched his shoulder he opened his eyes, those same eyes, calm and wise and full of courage, I first saw two years before. There was no sickness in them.

He raised his bony fingers in a victory sign.

That night I was startled from sleep at two in the morning. I'm not one normally given to premonitions, dreams, or divine appearances. I didn't want to wake my wife, so I left the bedroom and stretched out on the floor of our den. Then I had a vision. Not a dream, I was fully awake. I saw Troy dressed in a white robe, a skateboard tucked under his arm, the long black hair now shiny and full. He was walking across what appeared to be a flat expanse of desert, or perhaps a shallow lake. There were mountains in the background and a bright light was shining over his shoulder. When he reached the mid-distance he turned, waved to me, and smiled. Then he turned and walked toward the mountains, farther and farther away. He became a speck on the horizon, and then disappeared. Our phone rang. It was Sheila Lavelle, a social worker at the hospital who was a close friend of the Bylas family, calling to tell me that Troy had just died. She apologized for calling at 2:30 in the morning, but thought I would want to know. Of course, by then I already knew that Troy Bylas had left with courage to join the Holy Ones.

# GREGORI LAZARASHVILI

In 1976 I was on the staff of the Phoenix Indian Medical Center, a referral hospital for many of the Native American tribes of Arizona. I never imagined that in that capacity I would be called upon to rescue an eight-year-old boy in the Soviet Union.

It started with a phone call from Ollie Khursan, a college friend, who held a position with the Department of State in Washington, D.C. He knew I was working with the Public Health Service and came right to the point: Would I consider leaving for Russia in three weeks? I thought he was joking, but he was all business. An American exhibition was traveling to several cities in the Soviet Union interpreting American life through photography. It was a celebration of America's bicentennial year. Thirty graduate students, fluent in Russian and other Slavic languages, would spend a year in Russia. A doctor was needed for both medical and political reasons. The Cold War was at its height, and if a member of the American delegation became seriously ill and needed hospitalization, they could be detained indefinitely for "medical reasons." The doctor assigned to the exhibit had become ill himself, and the State Department needed a substitute for three months while the exhibit was in Tbilisi, the capital of the Soviet Republic of Georgia. He told me I would need to submit to a security clearance from the CIA. When cleared, my wife and I would receive State Department passports conferring full diplomatic immunity. If a member of the exhibit needed hospitalization, I was to accompany them to Helsinki, Finland, for treatment.

I reminded Ollie I spoke no Russian and informed him my wife was two months pregnant. I'd discuss the offer with her over the weekend, but it seemed like a long shot. He admitted it was an unusual last-minute request, but he reasoned since I was already working for the government, paperwork could be streamlined. He simply asked me to consider the offer. My wife was also taken aback by this unexpected proposition and was understandably concerned about our unborn child's health, but she was adventuresome. Her parents, who were world travelers, persuaded us to seize this unusual opportunity. It also helped we could receive supplemental food from the American Embassy in Moscow and would be in Soviet Georgia, where the Russian winters were less severe.

After the weekend I called Ollie and told him we'd decided to give it a go. He wasn't surprised. He'd already arranged for me to be assigned temporary duty to the State Department and for a doctor to serve in Phoenix during my absence.

We did our best to find maternity clothes suitable for a Russian winter, not abundant in Phoenix, while officials from the CIA interviewed us both for several hours. A week later they called, mostly satisfied with our meeting and their interviews with faculty from my high school, college, and medical school as well as with family and friends in New York, Michigan, and Arizona. The CIA Agents had one concern. They were curious. Was I a closet radical, a left-leaning revolutionary? They discovered I had a subscription to the *Akwesasne Notes*, a newspaper published by the Mohawk Nation from 1968-1992 that supported the agenda of AIM, the radical American Indian Movement. I explained I was sympathetic to the plight of Native Americans, but did not intend to over throw the Federal government! They were satisfied. We would be issued red diplomatic passports by the end of the week.

Incredibly, after two weeks of hectic preparation, Patty and I found ourselves sitting in the first class section of a Boeing 707 en route to Washington, D.C., for a two day protocol briefing by the State Department. We were informed there was a video bug in the mirror of our hotel room in Moscow and Tbilisi as well as several audio bugs. If any of the Russian-speaking Americans had an illness or emotional problem, I was to take them outside of the hotel for a discussion. The Russian secret police, then known as the KGB, would be aware of our every move.

We then boarded a plane from Washington, D.C., to Moscow, where we rested for two days and met with authorities at the American Embassy, where we were given diplomatic passports and more information about Tbilisi, Georgia, where we would be staying. We were advised about the protocol should an emergency arise. I would be given authority to fly a student to Helsinki, Finland, without permission from the Russians if a dire situation arose.

When we returned to the Hotel International every evening I would always hang my overcoat over the mirror. One time we ran out of toilet paper and the audio bugs worked to our advantage. I complained loudly that this would never happen in an American hotel. Five minutes later there was a knock on our door and a maid, employed in all likelihood by the KGB, arrived with two rolls of toilet paper. "Doktor Ameranski, you need dis for rhum?"

After our last visit to the American Embassy we were driven back to our hotel. The driver ushered us into a sumptuous limousine with wood paneling, a full bar, plush carpeting, and a spectacular audio system. He asked if we would like to take a slight detour through Sokolniki Park. We agreed. A light snow began to fall as we drove through a forest of larch and evergreen trees. It was like a scene from *Dr. Zhivago*.

The next day we left for Tbilisi on the Russian airline Aeroflot. We sat next to a woman who carried two chickens caged in her lap and shared pickled beets with us. As the months passed and it was more obvious that Patty was pregnant, she was frequently given snacks and treats from Soviet citizens, who love children.

On arrival in Tbilisi, we were met by the exposition director and taken to the exhibit site in Mushtaidi Park on the outskirts of Tbilisi. There we met the thirty American students who would be our companions for the winter. The exhibit, *Photography USA*, displayed photographs of people and places in the United States. At the end of the exhibit there was a working darkroom run by a specialist from the Smithsonian Institution. Charlotte Brooks, a highly-regarded portrait photographer for *Life Magazine*, had a studio next to the darkroom where she took portraits of randomly selected visitors to the exhibit with a 6 x 6 inch Polaroid view camera. Duplicates for the exhibit archives were made, the originals given to the visitors.

My wife greeted guests at the entrance, presenting each visitor with a little button pin, called a "snatchki" in Russian, similar to American political buttons. These pins carried the logo of our exhibit: a cut section of red, white, and blue photographic film twisted in a loop. The Russian-speaking Americans interpreted the exhibit, chatting with the visitors: our technician labored in the darkroom; and Charlotte took photographs while I mostly just waited for something to happen. An occasional student got laryngitis, a bladder infection, or menstrual cramps. One contracted venereal disease, a few were emotionally stressed, another cut her finger peeling a potato and needed stitches, but mostly I sat, read, and occasionally developed some of my own photographs in the darkroom that was adjacent to my "clinic," a space about the size of a large walk-in closet, fitted with an examining table, medicine cabinet, otoscope, ophthalmoscope, blood pressure cuff, and emergency devices that included an oxygen tank, respirator, defibrillator, and suction pump. Bandages, suture material, and most medicines needed to supply our clinic were provided by the American Embassy in Moscow. I was alerted in advance of an audio bug in the clinic. Sensitive issues with the American students would be discussed elsewhere.

Each day I was required to examine the office inventory, test the equipment, and complete a log book of this daily procedure. It seemed, at the time, like unnecessary bureaucracy, but I complied with the duties required. Why was all of this so important? The American students were in their prime, most in their twenties and thirties. This equipment, in all likelihood, would never be used, a waste of time, "government red tape."

Then, on a cold snowy morning in February my preparation, training, and organization paid off. Outside the exhibit hall an unusual mass of cold air settled over the city. Traffic sounds were hushed by a foot of new snow. Ominous gray clouds eclipsed the Georgian sun and temperatures dropped to 26° Fahrenheit. Despite the weather, long lines formed outside. The American, Russian, and Georgian flags, whipped by a stiff wind, snapped to attention over the exhibit.

Suddenly, the quiet erupted into bedlam, a mayhem of activity. The emergency exit door burst open and a hysterical elderly woman dressed in a heavy wool overcoat and fur hat that matched the grey clouds outside rushed toward me carrying the apparently lifeless body of a child. "Doktor Americonski?" I answered, "Da." She placed the cold, ashen body of her grandson into my arms. "Pajalste, DoKtor." (Please, Doctor). She made the Orthodox sign of the cross with her right hand, blessing me and the boy. Apparently she had been told an American doctor was on duty. She somehow managed to elude the KGB agents, members of the Soviet Secret Police, who monitored the exhibit.

A crowd of about 100 curious Georgians in the exhibit hall pressed closer, startled by the commotion and the deathly appearance of the child. I did not need to be told that the outcome from this encounter would have ramifications beyond the medical emergency at hand. I rushed the boy into our makeshift clinic, accompanied by the Russian-speaking assistant director of the exhibit.

The boy had a slow, weak pulse, a blood pressure of 80/50, and was hypothermic. I checked his airway and found his tongue inverted. He had what appeared to be aspirated food blocking his pharynx. I quickly removed this debris with my index finger, positioned him on his side, and performed a brisk Heimlich maneuver. He coughed and then vomited the rest of his morning breakfast. I placed a short plastic airway to secure his tongue and aspirated the remaining gastric fluid with the suction pump that I had loathed checking each day. He began breathing on his own. I supplied supplemental oxygen with a mask, wrapped his still frigid body in a thermal blanket, and delivered deep breaths of oxygen with an Ambu bag. Before long he opened his eyes, looked around and began to cry. He sat up and asked for his grandmother. The Russian-speaking assistant director, witness to these proceedings, assured him that his grandmother was waiting outside and he would be reunited with her when the doctor felt he was ready. The boy was lucid, but only remembered waiting in line with his grandmother. Then things went blank. He had been standing in line for over an hour. Meanwhile, the exhibit director had learned from bystanders he had an epileptic seizure. The seizure, his first, combined with the aspiration of food into his airway and hypothermia from the frigid weather outside, accounted for his precarious state on arrival. Examinations later that month by Soviet doctors diagnosed idiopathic epilepsy. As long as he took the prescribed medications of Dilantin and phenobarbital he would be fine.

When I opened the clinic door, the waiting crowd witnessed what they considered to be a miracle. An apparently lifeless eight-year-old boy now raised from the dead by an American doctor. The boy, smiling and running into the outstretched arms of his adoring babushka. Cheers. Toasts with brandy and vodka. Gregori Lazarashvili, a name akin to the Biblical Lazarus, from the Gospel of John, raised from the dead.

Word spread rapidly. When we took our lunch break in the restaurant adjoining the exhibit hall, several bottles of vodka and Georgian wine were sent to our table from local patrons who acknowledged their gift with a brief hand wave or nod of the head. There was even a rare bottle of Kinzmaruli, a rare red wine favored by Stalin. Luckily for both of us, the boy did not have an aneurysm or something more serious. I might have become a villain.

Instead, I was considered a hero. A "hero" who simply followed government protocol to ensure the emergency equipment was in working order and rendered care that might as easily been performed by an Eagle Scout with a First Aid merit badge, a diplomatic passport, and a bit of luck.

# STANISLAUS KOWALCZWYK

Some readers may think my experiences sound like a story from *National Geographic*. I can hear the comments from a hard-working general practitioner in Ohio: "Sure, any doctor can have adventures in Russia, working at an inner-city hospital, or on an Indian Reservation. But if Fisher had a real job in private practice as a PCP he'd have to deal with HMOs, PPOs, and DRGs. He'd be an LMD out the door ASAP with his PDR and SOAP notes on his ASS after a week*. In actuality, I worked as a partner at Consultants in Internal Medicine, a private medical group in Glendale, Arizona, for 29 years. There's been no shortage of adventure or inspiration. Let's begin with Stanislaus Kowalczwyk.

| | | | |
|---|---|---|---|
| *HMO: | Health Maintenance Organization | PDR: | Physicians' Desk Reference |
| PPO: | Preferred Provider Organization | SOAP: | Subjective, objective, assessment, plan |
| DRG: | Diagnostic Related Group | PCP: | Primary Care Provider |
| LMD: | Local Medical Doctor | ASS: | Ass |
| ASAP: | As Soon As Possible | | |

It's hard to say what caused the change in Stosh. According to his sister, Magda, it was not exactly a mid-life crisis; it was more gradual, more subtle. At first, the changes were noticed only by his family. Magda noted that around age 55, before coming to Arizona, Stosh became reckless and unpredictable, drinking, smoking, and eating to excess, talking too much, and driving his 1961 Buick LeSabre two-door convertible at breakneck speed. He was never mean. That was not his nature. He just didn't seem to care much about his own welfare or the future. True, his wife had died five years earlier and his kids were grown and on their own. He lived with his older sister, Magda. Nonetheless, he never seemed depressed.

There were no sudden mood swings. He was treasurer of the White Eagle Lodge and an usher at St. Wenceslaus Catholic Church. In 1986, when he was sixty one years old, his son and sister brought Stosh to my office hoping that I could help him. They were concerned about his failing health and also about his aberrant behavior. They related to me all of the following history.

Stosh's parents moved from Debnow, Poland, to the United States in 1928 when Stosh was two and his sister, Magda, four. The family entered the country through Ellis Island, as did so many other immigrants from Eastern Europe. They settled in Hamtramck, Michigan, in 1950, where the population was ninety percent Polish. The Kowalczwyks were one of ten million Polish American families that settled in America. They mostly took jobs in heavy industry, such as steel mills, coal mines, slaughterhouses, and manufacturing, and lived in communities like Hamtramck, where the radio stations, newspapers, and street signs were all in Polish. In 1930, the Polish population of Chicago was larger than that in Warsaw. Stosh did not speak English until the end of the third grade. There was no need; everyone spoke Polish. However, even if America had ethnic groups isolated by language and culture living in local communities—the Irish in South Boston, Italians in Brooklyn, Germans in Central Milwaukee—they were all patriotic Americans, cherishing new freedoms in their adopted country. In 1942, 16-year-old Stanislaus Kowalczwyk lied about his age and joined the U.S. Army to fight the Japanese invaders in the brutal jungle warfare of the South Pacific. At the war's end, private first class Kowalczwyk received an honorable discharge and returned home to Hamtramck. Stosh was proud of his military service, but he was furious about President Roosevelt's capitulation at Yalta, sacrificing his beloved homeland to Stalin and his Red Army thugs.

After the war, Stosh joined the United Auto Workers Union and labored on the production line at the General Motors assembly plant in Hamtramck. He spent the next forty years building Buicks and Cadillacs and raising his family. Near the end of his career, Stosh witnessed the ascendance of the Japanese auto makers—Nissan, Toyota, and Honda—as they outsold and outperformed General Motors and other American automobile companies. These were the very Japanese that Stosh had fought and defeated during World War II. Stanislaus Kowalczwyk was an angry man. The Japs had taken over the auto industry. Hamtramck, now only 25% Polish, had been invaded by Arabs and Blacks. Jobs and homes were being stolen from hardworking Poles.

Moreover, Stosh's arthritic knees were killing him, especially during the cold, damp Michigan winters. The extra 140 pounds he'd gained since the war didn't help either. He consumed enormous portions of babka (cake), kielbasa (sausage), kluski (potato dumplings), gulabki (stuffed cabbage), and chruschiki (fried dough with powdered sugar), washed down with gallons of Pabst Blue Ribbon beer. He no longer cared. One Sunday, Magda read a newspaper ad for homes in Sun City, Arizona. On an impulse, the Kowalczwyks decided to move to Arizona for sunshine and adventure. Stosh was tired of playing by the rules. Now, like his Western cowboy hero, John Wayne, he would make his own rules.

A 61-year-old chain smoking, 320-pound Stanislaus Kowalczwyk put Hamtramck in the rearview mirror of his Buick LeSabre and set out for Arizona with his sister, Magda, and his youngest son, Josef. En route they made a fateful stop to visit an old friend of Magda's living in Enid, Oklahoma. The personality changes noted years earlier by Magda were now fully developed and obvious to all. Stosh was a time bomb.

One evening, while watching a local newscast in Oklahoma, Stosh was introduced to the sport of noodling. Noodlers are usually men from the Southern states, large men who consume cases of beer beyond the need to slake their thirst. Then they submerge themselves along the banks of muddy rivers searching blindly with their hands for holes along the river's soft embankments, the hiding places for giant flathead catfish, some weighing 50 or 60 pounds. The catfish have no teeth, but clamp down hard on a noodler's hand and arm with powerful ancient instincts. The noodler, frequently with the help of his buddies, must lift the fish, still clamped to his arm, out of the water and onto the dry shore or into a boat—nothing complicated, but primitive. Unfortunately for some noodlers, the holes normally occupied by catfish are also home to other residents: snapping turtles, muskrats, beavers, snakes, and sometimes alligators. Stosh gave noodling a try, but he also gave the thumb, forth, and fifth fingers of his right hand to a snapping turtle. Oddly, Magda told me the injury seemed to invigorate him. He was strangely elated, even proud of the loss of his digits.

When we first met, Stosh was dressed in a floral Hawaiian shirt, cargo shorts, knee-high brown support hose, and white Reebok cross-trainers. He walked with a stiff, somewhat unsteady gait due to arthritic knees damaged from years of walking the cement floors of the GM assembly plant. His cigarette-scarred lungs revealed markedly decreased pulmonary function. The oxygen saturation of his blood was a dangerous 89 percent at rest. He had an outgoing, boisterous, but irreverent manner, a ruddy complexion, and a 52-inch waistline, his cargo pants secured with a section of Magda's clothesline. When he raised his right hand, the remaining two digits gave the macabre appearance of a papal blessing, an amputated sign of the benediction, otherwise seen on the five-fingered hand of the current Polish Pope, John Paul II.

Magda worried that Stosh wasn't taking his medication. He wanted freedom to go to bingo games at the Polish American Club, attend swap meets at Greyhound Park, and hang out with his buddies in downtown Glendale. During the next six months I simplified his medical regimen, obtained an oxygen concentrator for home use and a portable tank for outings. The necessary forms were completed and he was certified for an Amigo, a type of an electric portable mobility device (PMD) paid in full by Medicare and his United Auto Worker's insurance.

Stosh and I developed a friendly relationship, but he remained idiosyncratic, opinionated, brusque with our office staff, and less than compliant with his medical regimen. Imagine Archie Bunker with a Polish accent: "Dis gaz (oxygen) is goud stuff—keep me outta trouble. Never tink dey'd give me de 'lectric chair (referring to his portable mobility device)—taught dat vas joost for murders—get it, Doc? Ha! Now, if I could jus get dis goddamn ting to move like my Buick, I vould be in beezness." I smiled, glad to see that he was in better spirits. I checked his blood pressure, reviewed his lab reports, and scheduled a next appointment. At the time I didn't pay full attention to his comment about the portable mobility device—it was just talk.

About a month later I had a few extra minutes during lunch break, so I drove to a local Target store to get a few items for home. As I was leaving the store, my attention was drawn to a loud motorized sound and an enormous speeding object streaking through the Target parking lot. It was Stanislaus Kowalczwyk, riding his now souped-up Amigo and doing about 35 miles an hour. I waved him down. "Hey, Doc, vat you do, some shopping? Vat you tink of my 'lectric chair now, eh?" Stosh's son, Josef, worked in a lawnmower repair shop. He had helped Stosh retrofit the Amigo with a 3.5 horsepower Briggs and Straton engine, a centrifugal clutch, and larger wheels. I was speechless. I told Stosh the thing was top-heavy and dangerous. It was not meant to be driven like a Harley Davidson, especially given his enormous size and the location of the oxygen tank, separated from the sparkplug and gas tank by the width of a bungee cord. "You vory too much, Doc. All my pals, dey jealous bout my veels. I only open eet up on the straightway, never on the de curves. See ya later in veek, I got appointment." Stosh never made that appointment. He died several days later from a massive heart attack, one year before Poland became a free country under the leadership of Lech Walesa.

After the funeral I talked with Magda and Josef. We shared memories of Stosh and reflected on his idiosyncrasies. Magda felt her brother was fed up with America, disillusioned. The U.S. had abandoned Poland to Russia after the war and allowed the Japanese to take over the auto industry. The old neighborhoods were now ghettos riddled with crime. I recalled when Magda told me about Stosh's unexpected response to his noodling accident which paradoxically seemed to invigorate him with a sense of pride. Maybe he just felt more macho; perhaps now he had his own "war injury" to share with his buddies at the VFW post in Glendale. Josef, I believe, came nearest to the truth. He felt that his dad had always been a rebel, trying to adapt to a changing and often uncaring world. Perhaps what Magda and I considered risky and dysfunctional behavior was, for Stosh, the only way he could adapt and retain some pride. "If no von cares, den me, I don't care neither, joost vatch me."

I often advise my older patients *not* to "act their age," the opposite advice we gave our children on family road trips from the front seat of the car. Yet such advice was not necessary for Stosh. He went out on his own terms, a true Polski Amerykanin rebel, full of life, baka, kielbasa, and with a souped-up power chair and a half-full tank of oxygen.

# GINA ROLLEFSON

A well-dressed man gave his business card to our receptionist: "Peder Rollefson, Esq., Attorney at Law." He did not have an appointment and was not a patient, but said he wished to speak with Dr. Fisher. With a mixture of apprehension and curiosity I told our front office manager to escort the man to my office. A few minutes later a tall, blond man with Nordic features introduced himself. "Are you the Dr. Fisher who treated my wife, Gina, some years ago?" There was an uncomfortable pause before I answered. He could read my body language. "Yes," he said. "You must be that same Dr. Fisher."

Gina Rollefson first bounced into my office in 1981, my first year in private practice. She complained of a lingering pain and swelling in her left knee, the aftermath of a ski jumping accident. She also wanted to get better control of a chronic asthmatic condition and establish a relationship with an internist for any future medical needs. I was recommended by one of her neighbors. The swelling in her knee was due to a small tear in the medial meniscus, a cushion of cartilage between the femur and tibia. She was referred to an orthopedic colleague, and the defect easily repaired. Her asthma also responded rapidly to a simple regimen. Gina was in excellent health. She had an effervescent personality that was enhanced by a ready smile and large blue eyes that retained the color of Norwegian fjords, her native country.

During routine check-ups and occasional office visits for minor conditions over the coming years, we discovered we had a lot in common. Both she and her husband were raised in Michigan, my home state. The Rollefsons had two daughters, Kari and Tilla, age two and four, respectively, the same ages as our two daughters, Meredith and Brooke. We both loved Garrison Keillor's National Public Radio Show, *A Prairie Home Companion*, and enjoyed outdoor activities. We were both amateur birders. Gina was one of my first patients in private practice, and we were about the same age. In the coming years she shared many stories with me. The friendship that develops between doctor and patient is one of the treasures of primary care.

Gina Tisland was born in Norway in 1948. The Norwegian economy was slow to recover after World War II, but Gina's father, Lars, had an uncle in Green Bay, Wisconsin, not far from the famous Kingsford Charcoal plant in Michigan's Upper Peninsula. The uncle agreed to sponsor the Tisland's immigration and helped Lars find work at the charcoal plant, which was expanding to meet America's enthusiasm for backyard barbecues. Without much persuasion, the Tislands left Norway and arrived in Kingsford, Michigan, eight weeks later. Gina and her two brothers, Niels and Osten, attended school while Mrs. Tisland stayed home weeding the family garden, sewing, and helping the family adjust to their new country. She wanted her children to become "real Americans," but also insisted that only Norwegian be spoken in their home with family.

Kingsford was only a few miles from the famous Iron Mountain ski jump, the world's largest wooden ski jump. Mr. Tisland, a former ski jumper, drove his two sons and daughter there for lessons. It was Gina who had the most enthusiasm, nerve, and natural ability for this dangerous sport. She loved the whoosh of frigid air against her face and the magical lift under her skis, soaring like a winter raven. She practiced as often as her father could drive her to Iron Mountain, at least three days a week. When she couldn't get to the mountain, she practiced her graceful landings by leaping the fifteen steps that connected the Tisland kitchen to the basement below. Feather-light landings became her trademark

During the coming years, Gina won first place in the junior and senior competitions at Iron Mountain. At age fifteen she won the Junior National Championship. She loved the sport and wanted to take her skills to the next level. Mr. Tisland's sister, Olga, lived in Norway near the town of Holmenkollen. Gina still maintained Norwegian citizenship, and begged her parents to let her finish high school and practice for the team in Norway. Thanks to her mother's insistence that only Norwegian be spoken at home, she was still fluent in her native language. Naturally, the family had misgivings, but Gina was so insistent they finally agreed to let her move to Norway, live with Aunt Olga for the last two years of high school, and practice at the Holmenkollen ski jump. After twelve months, 17-year-old Gina Tisland qualified for a position on the Norwegian national team. In 1963, she traveled with the team to Innsbruck, Austria, where she won a silver medal in the World Federation Cup Championships. Women were not allowed to jump in the Olympics, held the next year at Innsbruck. After completing high school, Gina returned to the United States and was accepted at the University of Michigan, where she met her future husband, Peder Rollefson. Peder finished law school, married Gina, and left the snow and ice of Michigan for the sunny Southwest, where he joined a prominent Phoenix law firm. Gina, like her mother, stayed home to raise their two daughters.

Five years after we first met, Gina made an appointment. Her eyes told me something was wrong. Her oldest brother, Osten, was killed in an ice fishing accident. He had driven out onto Saginaw Bay in Michigan late in winter. That year there was an early thaw. Perhaps it was the heat and weight of Osten and his three buddies, fishing in an overheated shanty with two cases of beer and a kerosine heater, their Ford 350 pickup truck parked outside. The ice gave way and all four men, the shanty, and truck sank into the frigid water. Osten, a strong swimmer was the last to be seen by people on shore, helpless to reach him. He struggled to pull himself from the water, but those who witnessed the terrible scene reported that at the end, he seemed to "deflate" and calmly sank into the icy water of Saginaw Bay. Gina was devastated. I prescribed a mild tranquilizer and arranged for psychological counseling.

In the coming months, she improved. Someone who had not known her before Osten's accident probably wouldn't notice a change. It was as subtle as a small white cloud drifting over the horizon late on a winter afternoon. Gina was less spontaneous, more subdued. She began to make office appointments more frequently for a variety of somatic complaints. Tests were normal. Perhaps she was still grieving Osten's death. A month or so later she scheduled another appointment to evaluate lower abdominal pain, cramping, and mild back discomfort. Ten months before she had a normal gynecologic check-up, but I now detected a mass in her left ovary, confirmed by ultrasound. A biopsy revealed ovarian cancer. The uterus and both ovaries were removed. A single lymph node was positive for cancer. Gina was referred to an oncologist who supervised chemotherapy and radiation. Her long blond hair fell out in patches until she shaved her head and pulled on a light wool beanie from the Norwegian national ski team. Gina was no quitter.

I didn't see her for a few months as she was principally followed by the oncologists who monitored CA125 tumor markers, blood counts, chemistries, and periodic CAT scans. Then, one spring day in 1988, she scheduled an urgent visit for a persistent cough and breathlessness. Perhaps her asthma was acting up. When she arrived at the office, however, she was pale and had labored breathing. There were no breath sounds in her right hemithorax. An x-ray showed a large pleural effusion. I admitted her to the hospital and drained a liter of blood-tinged fluid from her chest. Pathologic examination of the fluid showed malignant cells. The oncologists were again consulted and a second round of chemotherapy was begun.

A month later I was on weekend call for our medical group making hospital rounds. I'd finished seeing our patients in the intensive care unit and medical floor and was doing a pre-operative evaluation for a surgeon when I had a nagging sensation I'd forgotten someone. I rechecked my printed patient list reviewing those patients I'd already seen that morning. No one was missing. Nonetheless, something, let's call it divine providence, made me return to the intensive care unit. It was an odd sensation I couldn't ignore. I looked again at the patient list on the board in the ICU. There were our patients: Brodsky, Bigley, Green, McCracken, Alvarez, and Rudolf. Then I saw it: Rollefson, Gina, cubical 8. The drapes were closed. I looked in and there was Gina, a pale skeleton struggling for breath, an oxygen mask in place, and a central venous line for medication and fluids. A chest tube and Foley catheter drained fluids into plastic bags that hung from the lower side rales of the hospital bed. She appeared to be sleeping. The nurse told me her husband and two daughters had just left for lunch. They'd been there all morning visiting with Gina. Then she opened her eyes, smiled, and with great effort shifted her weight in bed, patting the mattress for me to sit down. "Here I am," she whispered; it sounded Biblical. I believe that it was God's hand that led me to her bedside. She held my hand and said she knew I would come. She asked about my girls. We talked for a bit, and then she squeezed my hand. I recited the twenty third Psalm and the Lord's Prayer with her. The movements of her chest and abdomen slowed, and then, like her brother, Osten, who at the end effortlessly sank into the waters of Saginaw Bay, Gina seemed to relax and then submerged into the sheets and mattress of the hospital bed. She stopped breathing. The monitor showed ventricular fibrillation, then just a line, straight as a ski. A "do not resuscitate" order was in place. She died quietly. I waited for her family to return, but then there was an urgent page from the medical floor: "Dr. Fisher, STAT, Ocotillo 8. Dr. Fisher, STAT, Ocotillo 8." I had to leave. I never saw Mr. Rollefson or his girls again.

It was thirteen years later when Peder stopped by my office. He had an appointment with the orthopedic group at the end of our hallway. As he passed our office on the way out, he saw my name. This was not the office where I'd treated Gina, but a new office near another hospital. After he introduced himself I suggested we sit down for a few minutes, if he had the time. My medical assistant, Christi Cornish, brought coffee. Peder told me that six years after Gina's death he had remarried. He and his new wife had two boys, ages six and three. His holder daughter, Kari, had graduated from the University of Arizona and was in her second year of medical school at Johns Hopkins. She planned to do cancer research. His younger daughter, Tilla, graduated from the University of Michigan and married a young man in Lutheran Seminary. They lived not far from Kingsford. He told me how much he appreciated the care and attention I had given his wife Gina. The nurses told him I was there when she died. We shook hands and wished each other the best. It didn't seem appropriate for me to tell him my own wife, Patty, was in the last stages of terminal breast cancer. My involuntary tears that day were, in all likelihood, for both of these two strong women who deserved more time.

# LEONARD SANTOS
# & CAROLYN NICHOLS

## LEONARD

Remember those hippie buttons from the '60s: "Question Authority" and "Question Reality"? As a commander in the Commissioned Corps of the United States Public Health Service, I could hardly question authority, but I did begin to question reality when Leonard Santos, a previously healthy 28-year-old Mohave Indian was brought to the Phoenix Indian Medical Center with a mysterious ascending and progressive paralysis.

Late Friday afternoon, Leonard was finishing up at work and looking forward to the weekend. He had a date with his girlfriend, Mona, at a chicken scratch dance that night. The next day he'd get some help from his brother, a mechanic, because the carburetor on Leonard's 1968 Ford pickup was losing compression. When he awoke on Saturday morning, however, he noticed a dry cough and a peculiar taste in his mouth. By Monday, Leonard was exhausted.

His muscles were unusually weak, but, of course, over the weekend he'd finished working on the pickup and had helped his uncle stack some hay bales in the feed lot. By Wednesday, even Leonard recognized that something was terribly wrong. He had blurred vision, difficulty swallowing, and was so weak he couldn't get up from the breakfast table without assistance. His mother and Mona drove him to the nearby Indian Health Service Hospital in Parker, Arizona. His condition initially resembled Guillain Barre syndrome, but the rate of his symptom progression was unusually rapid. By then his condition had deteriorated even further. His arms and legs were nearly paralyzed and he was having trouble breathing. Because of the severity and rapid progression of his symptoms, he was transferred by airplane to the Phoenix Indian Medical Center, where I met him in the emergency department.

Leonard was considerably overweight, frightened, and breathing with shallow, anxious respirations. A brief examination revealed his deep tendon reflexes were absent and he could barely move his arms or legs, although he had normal sensation and was fully alert and aware of his precarious circumstances. There was no evidence of a tick bite or nuchal rigidity. He had not been ill during the weeks prior to this episode, nor could he recall any unusual circumstances, exposure, or illness. It was then that his mother, Elfreda Santos, spoke up. She remembered washing his clothes over the weekend and noticed a pungent, oily smell. Her son had taken a part-time job with a crop-dusting outfit in Bullhead City. It was fall, and time to defoliate the leaves from the cotton plants so the bolls could be harvested. It was Leonard's job to mix a viscous liquid compound, then fill the spray tanks of an open pit biplane with this product. Now Leonard remembered. He must have been distracted, thinking about the dance that night with Mona, or perhaps by the problems with his truck. He wasn't concerned when he splashed some of the liquid compound on his bare arms and soaked his T-shirt. He was busy, and wore the shirt all day, the excess moisture eventually evaporating into the dry desert air leaving an oily residue on the shirt and on Leonard's skin.

With this information, I called the Arizona Department of Agriculture and the Poison Control offices of the Maricopa County Health Department. The product that drenched Leonard Santos was Folex (merphos), an organophosphorus compound produced by the Exxon Petroleum Company. The product is rapidly absorbed through intact skin. Toxicologists recommended that Leonard receive injections of atropine and pralidoxime, antidotes for acute organophosphorus poisoning. However, because of delay from the time of exposure, it was not surprising that administration of these agents resulted in no discernible benefit. Soon he required ventilatory support, as his diaphragm and respiratory muscles began to fail. Complete paralysis ensued. He required intravenous feeding as he could no longer swallow. Tests of blood and spinal fluid were normal, except for a slightly elevated protein level in the spinal fluid.

Leonard was enormous, weighing more than 400 pounds, and completely paralyzed. We were concerned about pressure sores, so we ordered a special mattress to prevent decubitus ulcers from developing. We used a Stryker frame during the day. This device held Leonard like a hamburger between two buns: Leonard the meat, a soft pad underneath, and on top, the buns. When "the buns compressed the meat," Leonard could be rotated 180 degrees and thoroughly inspected from top to bottom to be sure no bedsores were developing and proper bathing could be facilitated. After two weeks of therapy, there was still no change in his weakened condition, although by the fourth week he regained enough strength to initiate inspiration with assistance from the respirator.

The Mohave Indians are traditionally quiet and mild-mannered, accepting the hardships of desert life and cultural disruptions, first from the Spanish and later from American settlers seeking gold. Nonetheless, I could tell the family was understandably upset and anxious about Leonard's condition. Elfreda asked what they could expect. Mona wondered if Leonard would improve. If so, how long would it take? There was little written about delayed organophosphorus toxicity, and nothing regarding toxicity in humans from the product Folex.

With the help of our medical librarian (this was in the days before the internet), I learned that a scientist in England, Dr. M.K. Harbeldown, was doing research on Folex toxicity, using chickens as his experimental model. I arranged for a telephone conference with the doctor, an ocean and continent away in his laboratory at Chelmsford, approximately thirty miles northeast of London. Dr. Harbeldown explained his experimental design. He strapped chickens into a device that resembled, to my imagination, a Ferris wheel, like those found in amusement parks across America. The chickens, eight to a wheel, were held in little canvas sling-seats and self-fed with troughs placed before them. Their legs were held in extension with tiny braces. The Ferris wheel was on a timer. As the wheel turned, each chicken had their feet immersed in Folex for varying amounts of time when they reached the bottom of the wheel. Then, after varying intervals of exposure, the birds were sacrificed and the nerve cells in their legs examined under a microscope to assess the degree of nerve damage. I asked Dr. Harbeldown, on Leonard's behalf, the most telling question: "Had any of the chickens recovered?" The doctor was quiet, pausing in contemplation. I imagined him filling his briar pipe with a dark tobacco, tamping it down and lighting the pipe bowl before he answered in a crisp British accent, "One." "One?" I asked. "Yes." Dr. Harbeldown was a thorough researcher, although frugal with words. Recovery, he explained, was not part of his experimental design. However, a single chicken had escaped from his little sling during one of the experiments and hid in the laboratory for several weeks before being discovered. He recalled that the chicken was difficult to capture, though it did seem, upon reflection, to have some problems with balance and agility. One escaped chicken. Not much information for the Santos family. I thanked Dr. Harbeldown and returned to the intensive care unit where I was struck by the odd resemblance of Leonard in the Stryker frame and the circular device described by the British doctor to test his chickens.

With total parenteral nutritional supplementation (TPN), careful monitoring of fluid and electrolyte balance, frequent turning, attention to respiratory and digestive function, Leonard gradually improved. After eight weeks he could stand with assistance. By the twelfth week he could brush his hair, drink coffee from a cup, and swallow. After three months he could walk with a broad-based gait out the doors of the Phoenix Indian Medical Center and into his truck, the carburetor now performing like new. Mona drove him home to the reservation. During the long hospital stay, the Mohave tribe helped Leonard win a lawsuit for lost wages and damage against the owners of the crop duster. Exxon, the manufacturer of Folex, now has a large warning label printed on its container instructing thorough washing of any skin exposed to the product and immediate removal of contaminated clothing. Two months later, Leonard Santos was hired to work in the maintenance department at the Bullhead City Hospital. I later received, by certified mail, a certificate signed by the members of the Mohave Tribal Counsel accepting me as an honorary member of the Mohave tribe.

After this encounter, I searched the medical records for the past ten years to identify patients admitted to the Phoenix Indian Medical Center with the diagnosis of Guillain Barre syndrome. Nine cases were found. Eight patients lived near cotton fields and their hospital admission was during the time when defoliants were commonly applied to the cotton fields of Arizona by crop dusters. Their exposure would have been less intense than Leonard's, but the association of Leonard's condition and aerial spraying was brought to the attention of the Arizona Department of Health and to the Tribal Councils in exposed areas.

# CAROLYN

Have you ever had a day when, upon arising, you feel out of place, a bit peculiar? Perhaps it's the change from daylight savings time, a leap year, a poor night's sleep. Usually it's nothing that one can name, just a sensation that might color the events of the coming day. I experienced such a day on a gray morning in 1984, three years after I joined a medical group in private practice. I decided to begin riding my bike to work. I don't use earphones while riding, I just pedal and give my mind a chance to relax. Maybe that's what caused my sense of displacement. Perhaps I was hyperaware of my surroundings.

I traveled the smooth, paved bikepath alongside the Arizona Canal, an irrigation project that delivers water to the rapidly growing population of Phoenix. I knew the canal followed the same path as one built by the ancient Hohokam people, who inhabited the valley that is now Phoenix, 1000 years before the arrival of Christopher Columbus. Ironically, a huge bronze statue of Columbus was now just visible to me in the early morning light in front of the Italian American Club.

A few miles down the canal I found a palo verde tree with more than a hundred peach-faced lovebirds, little eight-inch parrots with yellow bills, peachy-cream faces, green bodies, and iridescent blue wings, perched in the branches. The birds, native to Africa, had escaped from their cages and have now established feral breeding colonies in Arizona. Odd, parrots in the desert.

I may also have been distracted by thoughts of a ride a few days earlier when I witnessed policemen pull the bloated body of an elderly man from the canal. Two miles further along the path I passed an amusement park. Floodlights illuminated the empty park in the early morning darkness, loudspeakers still playing calliope music, a pipe organ slightly off-key, a requiem, perhaps, for the dead man I'd seen earlier in the week. Near the amusement park is the city dog pound. The plaintive howls from some of the dogs I heard on the morning ride to work would be silenced forever by the time I made the return trip home that evening. Maybe it was everything—the departed Hohokam culture, Columbus in bronze, the escaped lovebirds, the dead man, the empty amusement park, the calliope music, the imprisoned dogs— all mixed up like mental confetti, like a scene from a Federico Fellini movie. Whatever were my random mental associations, I arrived at work unsettled. I needed to clear my mind before I began a full day of scheduled patients, but I was not afforded that luxury.

It was on that morning Carolyn Nichols, a new patient, was signing in at the front desk when I arrived. She complained of shortness of breath, wheezing, facial swelling, and abdominal pain. On the walk down the hallway to the examining room, she collapsed, with audible wheezing and rapid, shallow respirations. Her skin turned ashen blue. Our nursing staff brought the crash cart and called 9-1-1. An IV was started, pulse oximetry checked, and we began oxygen by mask while also administering subcutaneous epinephrine, intravenous diphenhydramine, and solunedrol. Soon the paramedics arrived. Her condition had improved considerably. Nevertheless, I accompanied her in the ambulance on a short drive from our office to the hospital. When she was secure in her hospital bed, alert, and breathing more easily, I noted she had no skin rash or any other unusual physical findings except for some residual periorbital edema, lip swelling, and mild expiratory wheezing.

Now, out of danger, she told me she had worked at the same school as a third grade teacher and lived alone with her cat (same cat, same apartment) for the past eight years. She had no dietary changes, but she was never able to wear costume jewelry, as it caused swelling and itching where it contacted her skin. These symptoms, however, were getting much worse. She couldn't come in contact with any metal. She ate with plastic utensils and wore cotton gloves when she opened doors, used her vacuum, or worked with gardening tools. She did mention her gallbladder had been removed about three months prior to this admission, and she felt her symptoms had worsened during the weeks since that surgery. Today's episode, she reasoned, may have been precipitated by her thoughtless use of a metal safety pin to fasten her blouse which had lost a button. She was afraid of being late for her appointment.

A chest x-ray was taken and laboratory studies ordered. Everything was normal. Abdominal films showed eight metallic clips in her right upper quadrant. We consulted the operative report. The stainless steel clips used during her gallbladder surgery were produced by the 3M Company, Minnesota Manufacturing and Mining (the same company that makes Scotch Tape). The clips contained ten percent nickel. A patch test with 2.5 percent nickel sulfate caused immediate swelling of her skin and audible wheezing. The findings were discussed with a surgeon, and after some persuasion, he agreed to remove the clips from Carolyn's abdomen. After removal of the clips, for the first time since they were implanted, her condition improved dramatically. She still had to be careful with costume jewelry and prolonged exposure to metals containing even trace amounts of nickel, but she could now perform normal daily chores without special precautions. After reviewing the literature, I discovered that pacemakers, intrauterine devices, foreign bodies from injuries, and certain prosthetic devices have also been implicated in allergic reactions. Perhaps our suspicions should have been alerted much earlier, when Carolyn first signed her name as a new patient at our reception desk: Carolyn NICHOLS.

Louis Pasteur believed "chance favors the prepared mind." Delayed neurotoxicity from an organophosphorus compound and extreme nickel sensitivity are not routinely encountered in medical practice. Experience and familiarity with more common conditions help to alert the practitioner to the unusual. Carolyn had only minor problems with her allergy in the years to come. Leonard made a complete recovery. The case reports of both patients were published in the *Journal of the American Medical Association*.

# GILBERT TAFOYA

Former Marine Captain Gilbert Tafoya had a receding hairline that was about to merge with a bald spot on the crown of his head. The hair loss was not so much from advancing age as from the potency of the male hormone, testosterone, that caused hair to eject from his scalp the way bullets ejected from his M1 rifle at the Korean battle at Inchon. At age 62, the tattoo of the Marine motto, Semper Fi, inked on his right upper arm, was beginning to fade, its margins less distinct from the surrounding dermis, but Tafoya himself was not fading— quite the opposite. At office appointments to control blood pressure and cholesterol, his manner was always "take charge, can do." He habitually greeted me with an extra-firm handshake and intense eye-to-eye contact. His only outward idiosyncrasy was the omnipresence of a small pocket radio carried in his shirt pocket or clipped to his belt that piped loud mariachi music through portable earphones directly to Gilbert's eardrums, but with such volume the music was audible to anyone nearby. Ever since he returned from Korea he listened non-stop to mariachi. The music relaxed him. It was his therapy.

His demeanor was otherwise serious and mostly humorless. He'd grown up on a dairy farm in Buckeye, Arizona, where, after the Korean conflict, he returned. His parents had relocated to San Diego in retirement, so Gilbert moved into the old home, continued the family dairy business, married his high school sweetheart, and raised a family. His children were doing well. He and his wife, Mimi, were happy and the dairy business was thriving. Then, one morning, while changing the oil filter on his tractor he experienced the sudden onset of chest pain, nausea, sweating, and lightheadedness. Mimi found him sitting on a hay bale and called 9-1-1. Gilbert Tafoya was having an acute myocardial infarction- a heart attack.

He was given nitroglycerine, aspirin, intravenous lidocaine, and oxygen by paramedics and rushed to Maryvale Samaritan Hospital, where I admitted him to the cardiac care unit. A cardiology consultant performed coronary angiography, which showed complete blockage of the right anterior coronary artery and ninety-percent blockage of the circumflex and left anterior descending coronary arteries. The vessels were too narrow for an angioplasty, so a three-vessel coronary artery bypass graft was performed by a thoracic surgeon. He was given blood thinners, instructions for cardiac rehabilitation, and continued with therapy to regulate blood pressure and cholesterol levels.

After a few weeks he was back on his feet. I'll never forget his first visit to the office after the heart attack. Velcro bands secured ten pound weight belts around his ankles. The right sleeve of a pale blue T-shirt, displaying the logo of a local irrigation company, was rolled just enough to secure a pack of unfiltered Camel cigarettes, exposing the legs and talons of the Eagle tattoo. He sported a green and yellow John Deere tractor cap with pins of the American Flag and the Marine Corps, one on each side. He walked with the assurance of an alpha male. When he removed the ankle weights for his check-up, he moved like Michael Jackson doing a moon walk. His whole demeanor was similar to the advertisements seen in *Popular Mechanics*, the ones at the end of the magazine, extolling body-building programs so bullies won't kick sand in your face at the beach. "Great to see ya, Doc. How's life treating you?" He remained on the offensive, deflecting any questions about his recent hospital stay or tobacco use. Yes, he was taking his medicines. Now, in the office, only two weeks after hospital discharge, he reminded me of Jack Palance, who dropped to the ground and did twenty pushups during the 1984 Oscar ceremonies.

I asked about his rehab program. Gil knew what was best for him; he had developed his own regimen. He owned a one-year-old pit bull puppy he carried in his arms up and down the half-mile stretch from his farm to the main road. It gave new meaning to taking the dog for a walk. He'd gotten the idea from a book he'd read during cardiac rehabilitation about the Greek warriors. He contended the Spartans gained strength by carrying a newborn calf in their arms. As the calf grew, so did the strength of the Spartans. By the time the calf was fully grown, the Spartans, gradually accustomed to the increasing weight, could now carry the full grown bull! He didn't understand when I asked him if the Spartans could also "throw the bull" or examine bovine excrement. As I said, Gilbert Tafoya was humorless.

In the coming months and years, Gilbert grew stronger and seemed to have regained his prior vitality. He went elk hunting with his buddies, accompanied Mimi to yard sales, went fishing in his bass boat at Lake Pleasant, and called square dances for the Buckeye 4H Club.

Then he had a second heart attack.

He had become less meticulous with his medication, smoked two packs of the unfiltered Camels daily and was liberal with his use of smokeless tobacco when he was around gasoline or propane. He knew the worrisome signs. This time, however, his hospitalization required no significant surgical interventions, just resumption of his prescribed medications and elimination of tobacco. Now he was on a mission. He said he'd give up tobacco and join the YMCA, where he worked out on a treadmill and with free weights at least four days a week. This regimen was supplemented by "walking the dog" and a blended concoction of his own invention, consumed in his kitchen before leaving for workouts. It consisted of two raw eggs, chopped spinach, fat free yogurt, skim milk, Omega-3 fatty acids, vitamin C with bioflavonoids, Coenzyme-Q, brewer's yeast, and two teaspoons of emu oil. Describing this program, he told me, "Doc, I've never felt better. With all of these supplements I piss the color of my kid's old school bus!" Then, at the end of his checkup he asked, "Hey, Doc, want to come to a tractor pull in Buckeye this Saturday? You can bring your family." I thanked him, got the details and directions, and told him I would check with my wife. I had never been to a tractor pull. On the other hand, nor had I ever attended a public execution.

A tractor pull would not be high on the list of weekend activities chosen by most wives, and mine was no different. She politely declined. My daughters, age ten and eight at the time, were more enthusiastic. They would rather go to the zoo, but maybe if they got to drive a tractor that would be fun. I was glad they came, because my wife would have some time to herself and my kids would be exposed to something different. Besides, I felt I needed to show up since Gilbert's enthusiasm was so infectious. He'd been my patient for ten years, and it was hard to decline his invitation. It was only three weeks since his most recent MI, but how stressful was a tractor pull? I was optimistic, but in retrospect, I was in denial.

He greeted the three of us warmly, standing next to his red pickup at the entrance to his farm. In the bed of the truck was a milking machine in need of repair, some canned goods for a church food drive, an empty acetylene tank used for welding, and some sewing material Mimi asked him to drop off at the 4H Center. He told the girls to hop into the truck bed. I'd sit up front with Gilbert and he'd take us on the back road a mile or two to the arena. It was safe, he reassured us.

Ironically, the sport of tractor pulling began without tractors. Horses pulled down old barn doors that needed replacement. The doors were placed flat on the ground, attached by a chain to a team of horses. Weights, typically hay bales, were loaded on top of the door. The goal was to see how much weight a horse, and later, a tractor could pull. Tractors had low gear ratios for maximum power, but now, even tractors have been "souped-up" for the limited attention of today's audiences, outfitted with jet engines like the monster trucks that perform at state fairs. The pull in Buckeye, however, was more traditional, showcasing regular farm equipment, moving slowing and dragging heavy loads, while family, relatives, and the uninitiated—like ourselves—stood at the edge of the arena watching respectfully from a distance.

We'd been at the arena in Buckeye for about three hours. My daughters wore floral cotton sundresses that stood out among the jeans, work shirts, and boots like candelabra at a fish fry. They tried to make eye contact with me, their eyebrows raised in supplication: "Ready to go, Dad? How much longer are we going to stay?" I told them Gilbert's tractor was next. They glared.

Gilbert drove his John Deere into the ring, the chain and wooden sled secured to the back of his tractor. He would pull in the tractor's lowest gear while others gradually added weight to the sled. The tractor moved with his expert touch as much as a giant sequoia might grow in a year, so slow, that to the untrained eye there was no perceptible motion at all. Then his engine stalled. It was not his carelessness, but something wrong with the engine. Gil dismounted, removed a wrench from a toolbox next to the seat, and crawled underneath the John Deere. I noted a cigarette now dangled from the corner of his mouth. As he lifted the heavy wrench to disengage a bushing from underneath the tractor, the headset jack from his pocket radio was disconnected and mariachi music flooded the arena. One of the belts needed tightening, and in this position it required considerable force. Even at the distance of fifty yards I could see heavier puffs of cigarette smoke wafting from beneath the tractor. It had been three weeks since his heart attack. I watched Gilbert's chest heaving and imagined the eagle wings tattooed on his left biceps were about to fold. Was this a sign? Would Tafoya's body be added to the load on the tractor sled, further augmented by his doctor frantically performing CPR as it exited the muddy arena? Both of my daughters were oblivious to the unfolding drama, and now asked aloud, "Dad, can we go?"

In the end, all went well. Gilbert fixed the problem with the tractor and was awarded a ribbon for second place. He was okay with that. He'd do better next time. Gilbert gave my girls little rings he'd made from horseshoe nails which he'd heated and bent over an anvil. My daughters were polite, but a father can usually read a daughter's mind: "No ruby, no diamond, three hours in the sun, no ride on a tractor, and our reward is a bent nail?" I appreciated Gilbert's kind gesture and his enthusiasm for tractor pulls. At the same time, as his doctor, I realized that despite ominous warnings—heart attack, stroke, the return of curable cancers—many people develop habits that may be impossible to change. As doctors, we have to accept this recalcitrance as part of life, something over which we have little control. These were my thoughts as I drove back to Phoenix with my daughters in the back seat, ominously quiet. This would be their last tractor pull. I hoped that it wouldn't be Gilbert's.

# SIDNEY RHEINSTEIN

In April 1969, the New York City Public Schools were paralyzed by a teacher strike. The protest was soon joined, in sympathy, by some of the city's nurses, which resulted in staffing shortages at many hospitals. At the time I was a third-year medical student at Columbia University College of Physicians and Surgeons. Third and fourth year medical students were offered temporary positions at $15.00 an hour to work as private duty nurses—a lot of money for a medical student. I could work the 10 p.m. to 8 a.m. shift, when the patients were usually sleeping. I'd be able to catch up on my studies or nap. How hard could a private duty nursing job be anyway? Little did I know I would be doing little studying or napping when I signed up. Luckily I was caught up on my studies, because I received an unexpected education during my brief career as a nurse.

I was assigned to a patient in the Harkness Pavilion, a section of the Columbia Presbyterian Medical Center reserved for foreign dignitaries, celebrities, and people of means. Unlike the open ten-bed wards to which I'd become accustomed as a medical student, all the rooms in the Harkness Pavilion were private. They were not really rooms, but suites, which to my imagination resembled a fashionable downtown Manhattan men's club. Doors, paneling, bookshelves, a writing desk, and armoire were made of luxurious mahogany with brass fittings. Pictures of English fox hunting scenes decorated the walls. Oddly enough, this particular room, #210, would in fact become a men's club of sorts.

When I first entered this luxurious room, I thought my patient was asleep, so I sat down quietly in an overstuffed leather chair next to his bed without speaking. I'd been instructed by the charge nurse to check the patient's intake and output, keep an eye on the schedule of his medication, check his intravenous line and Foley catheter, and record vital signs at hourly intervals. He had a heart condition and a terminal illness for which he was receiving palliative treatment, but the patient, Sidney Rheinstein, was not asleep. He was sizing me up. I sat in the leather chair taking notes from my physiology textbook, occasionally looking up. At times I imagined I saw one of his eyes quickly shut. After twenty minutes, he spoke to me in an alert, calm, clear voice: "If you are here to be my nurse, maybe we should be introduced. My name is Sidney Rheinstein. What's yours? Fisher? Jeffrey Fisher? Are you Jewish? No. Well, that's okay. Are you a medical student? What year? Where did you go to college? Princeton!" His eyes lit up. He sat bolt upright in bed, held out his hand, and said, "Sidney Rheinstein, class of '07." I countered, "Jeffrey Fisher, class of '65." Fifty-eight years of Princeton graduates separating us, now a reunion in Room 210. I was still being examined. "What was your major? Biology? I guess they filled you in on my history. Pretty sad, huh, my condition? Well, maybe 81 years isn't so bad for an economics major and a stockbroker who lived through the Crash of 1929 and two world wars. Tell me more about yourself."

I wasn't inclined to talk about myself, but at his prompting I told him I had grown up in New York but moved to Detroit in the sixth grade when my father accepted an executive position with the Ford Motor Company. I attended public grade schools, but then went to Cranbrook School, a private school for boys, where I played sports and was active in student government. I loved animals and the outdoors and nearly died of hypothermia on a fishing trip to Canada with one of my best friends from college. No, I didn't go into the field of medicine for money, but I could use the extra cash now. That's why I'd decided to do some private-duty nursing. I had to work hard in medical school, but I loved it. Then he said, "Do you know what makes people boring? When they talk about themselves and you want to talk about yourself." Then he paused. "Sorry, I didn't mean you, Fisher. I was asking you questions about yourself. That's different." "Well," I said, "tell me about yourself." And he did.

After graduating from Princeton, Mr. Rheinstein and a college friend sold stocks on the curb before he purchased a seat on the New York Stock Exchange in 1909 with $75,000 that he inherited from his father and money he had earned the previous two years. He told me, with some humility, he had traded more individual shares of stock than any other living member of the stock exchange. He had worked five days a week for the past 51 years.

Mr. Rheinstein was a specialist, trading in Lehman Brothers, Paramount Pictures, General Foods, Phillips Petroleum, and

American Metals. He ate lunch every day on the seventh floor of the New York Stock Exchange Luncheon Club at 11 Wall Street, sitting at one of two tables with his friends. He enjoyed two tumblers of scotch with lunch and savored spirited discussions with his cronies. In 1941 (two years before I was born) he was elected as a member of the Board of Governors of the Stock Exchange. Talking with Mr. Rheinstein was better than any history course taught at Princeton. It was living history.

He was a close friend of Allan Lehman, the founder of Lehman Brothers. It was Mr. Lehman who asked him to be a specialist for his company. He was proud of being an American and proud of his contribution to the country. He told me stock traders paid more tax to the United States government than any other class of people. America would not have won either the First or the Second World War without the help of big American corporations like US Steel, General Motors, General Electric, Westinghouse, Allied Chemical, and Union Carbide, who themselves received financing from the Stock Exchange.

Mr. Rheinstein recounted his experiences from that fateful "Black Tuesday," October 29, 1929, when the Stock Market crashed (the Big Wind). Even on that day, Sidney Rheinstein earned $250,000 with his partners while other investors lost everything. Weeks before the crash, Mr. Rheinstein felt the market was overvalued and sold many of his holdings. Normally a "bull," he became a "bear." He also admitted luck played a role. He always tried to diffuse tension with humor. For example, he told me a week before the crash two Jews met outside an office building on Wall Street. One said to the other, "Mein gott, I hodt a terrible thing happen to me today. Mein doctor told me I haf diabetes at 42." The other answered, "You should vorry. I haf Chrysler at 104!" He told me that in his opinion a stock market crash like the one of '29 was possible anytime in the future.

Mr. Rheinstein had a simple but practical philosophy of life. The only material things he considered worth their value were good shoes and a good mattress. As far as personal matters, he regularly smoked two cigars a day, only primo panetellas imported from Cuba. He drank two single malt scotches with lunch and steamed in a Turkish bath for an hour between the morning and afternoon trading sessions. For breakfast, he drank soup instead of coffee. His sister, Alice, introduced him to a Norwegian technique of slow, deep breathing exercises akin to yoga or Buddist meditation, which he continued to practice for the rest of his life thirty minutes each morning after his soup. He and his beloved wife had rocking chairs (with shortened rockers so guests wouldn't trip) installed around their dining room table in Long Island. Rocking, he believed, aided digestion. It was late and we were both tired, but invigorated by the conversation. I suggested he get some sleep while I attended to my nursing duties.

For the next four nights, Mr. Rheinstein and I discussed a variety of subjects, from the value of organized religion to the nature of friendship, like two college freshman engaged in a dormitory bull session. More importantly, I sensed he wished to be my mentor, allowing me to benefit from his life experiences. On the fourth night he offered me a Havana cigar and two fingers of single-malt Scotch whiskey. I worried it might seem unprofessional to accept, but he seemed to want the fellowship. The rooms were ventilated to the outside, and smoking was permitted in the hospitals in 1968. While we were conversing, smoking, and sipping our Scotch, the head nurse entered the room. She was appalled. I received a stern reprimand about smoking and drinking while on duty. She said she would notify the dean of students about my unprofessional conduct. I was no longer welcome in the Harkness Pavilion. The next morning I met with Dr. George Perrera, dean of the medical school, to explain my behavior. By coincidence, Dr. Perrera was also a Princeton graduate. After hearing my explanation of the companionship that Mr. Rheinstein sought and a description of the duties I performed as a private-duty nurse, he was reassured. Smoking a cigar and enjoying a Scotch at the request of a dying patient was the right thing to do. He would call the director of nursing, a longtime friend, and have me reinstated. Mr. Rheinstein himself insisted I be allowed to return, since he was paying the bills!

This experience did, however, give me insight into the immense responsibility given to nurses. Doctors make rounds and visit a patient for only fifteen to twenty minutes a day. The nurse is at the bedside for eight hours or more, providing the patient with emotional and physical support without the benefit of Scotch or a smoke. In the coming years I always respected the care given to my patients by skilled nurses when I was absent from the bedside.

At the end of the week, I told Mr. Rheinstein I had to leave town for a few days. I'd be back soon. He told me he'd enjoyed our conversations immensely, they had raised his spirits more than I could imagine. He also requested I continue to be his nurse, if I had the time. When I returned, after a few days absence, I found room 210 occupied by an elderly woman sitting in a wheelchair. The nurses told me Mr. Rheinstein died the night after I left, but he had instructed them to give me a package. It was an autographed copy of a book he'd written about his career on the New York Stock Exchange.

Sidney Rheinstein was a remarkable man. He had the good sense to balance both his professional and personal lives, enjoying a vigorous and successful business career, yet finding time for personal relaxation with his family and friends. I thought of Sidney Rheinstein recently, during the economic turmoil of 2008 and the demise of Lehman Brothers. He probably wouldn't have been surprised. He told me one night, "Credit is suspicion asleep." He probably would have advised Lehman Brothers to abandon their high-risk real estate derivatives. This advice would be offered only, of course, after he'd finished his Scotch, a Cuban cigar, and a Turkish bath with his friends.

# ROBERT J. FISHER

During World War II, my father was a lieutenant in the United States Navy aboard the aircraft carrier U.S.S. *Salvo Island*. I was born in 1943. When I was about two years old I asked my mother, "Where's Daddy?" Her answer shocked me. Perhaps she phrased it differently, but this is what I remember: "Jeff, your father is fighting Germans so our world will be safe."

I felt very safe in Syracuse, New York, even if surrounded by Germans. I lived with my mother, grandparents, and an extended family of great aunts and uncles. My grandmother was the youngest of four married sisters. I was the only child at home. My older cousins were away at college or jobs. We were a close family that gathered often: Benners, Heitzmans, Fondrichs, Homeyers, and Schlossers. Aunt Elsie played the piano. On Sundays, the sisters harmonized Lutheran hymns with an occasional rousing Bavarian drinking song thrown in. My Uncle John, a math teacher, taught me to count: "eing, zwei, drei, vier, fünf ..." Uncle George, a retired fireman, dabbled in viticulture.

He had a trellis of concord grapes in his backyard from which he made a sweet table wine pressed and aged in his cool basement. The wine was bottled and corked in green Sunkist prune juice bottles with the original labels steamed off in their bathtub, a scary tub with the four corners supported by what appeared to be baseballs gripped in the claws of a monster. Elsie printed new labels and glued them to the bottles: "New York State Concord Sweet Table Wine, Vineyard of George Homeyer, Syracuse, New York." Later in life, during medical school, I remembered the hundreds of empty prune juice bottles lining the shelves of Elsie and George's basement. In order to consume the enormous quantity of prune juice required to provide her husband with bottles, Aunt Elsie must have had an abiding love for George or else a serious decrease in gastrointestinal motility. In either case, the wine was corked, aged, chilled, and served at our Sunday gatherings. Even a two-year-old boy was allowed to partake, which often led to a sound nap afterward.

One afternoon, after a nap, Mom told me someone was here to see me. She carried me into the parlor where, still somewhat groggy from the wine, I found a giant standing at attention in a dark-blue uniform. He wore a white hat appearing to have scrambled eggs on its black brim. I could see my reflection in the high polish of his shoes. In retrospect, it may have been the sight of my metal leg braces that got the giant's attention. I had to wear them for tibial torsion, a correctable abnormality of my lower legs. More likely, it was regal bearing of an overindulged mildly intoxicated two-year-old with an air of entitlement. He was not pleased to learn of my fondness for wine and ability to count in German. He reached down to pick me up. Mom told me this was my dad. I cried and hit him with my little fists, unable to kick because of the leg braces. I reasoned he probably was here to fight more Germans and kidnap me. I was so distraught he was forced to hand me back to my mother. I think my father and I just got off to a bad start, certain inherent misunderstandings between a long absent 27-year-old Navy lieutenant and his pampered two-year-old son.

As I grew older, Dad and I shared a mutual respect. He had a good sense of humor, was outgoing, sociable, and intelligent. He was also driven. He had a quick temper and often relied on sarcasm to make a point. He expected a lot from himself and from others, perhaps because of a competitive relationship with his own father, a plumber, who at age fifty taught himself Spanish with the help of tapes mailed from the Berlitz Language School. My grandfather wrote long letters in Spanish to a pen-pal in Santiago, Chile, and also wrote letters in Spanish to my father and my uncle Joe during the war. They had to find a Mexican or a Puerto Rican in their units to read the words written by their own father. Why it was so important for my grandfather to learn Spanish, I'll never know. To my knowledge, the Hispanic population of Ashland, Ohio, who needed a plumber in the 1930s could not have been sizeable.

Dad also pushed himself to excel, to be better than his father and two brothers, better than everyone at anything. A first team All-American high-school basketball player, he was admitted to Syracuse University on basketball and academic scholarships—full ride. Nevertheless, he shoveled coal and washed dishes for the Kappa Kappa Gamma Sorority House to earn spending money. It was there he met my mother. After graduating Phi Beta Kappa and marrying my mother, he was accepted as a graduate student in English at Harvard University, where he studied and worked as a teaching assistant. When

Pearl Harbor was attacked by the Japanese, he left school and enlisted in the US Navy. During the war years he had time to reconsider his profession. An academic tenure would be one of relative poverty, much like his father's plumbing business. Instead, in sales he could make some real money. After an honorable discharge from the Navy, he was hired by a New York advertising agency located at 30 Rockefeller Plaza, with an office on the 14th floor of the RCA Building overlooking the skating rink and the famous Christmas tree. Eight years later, he was offered a position as advertising and sales manager for the Ford Motor Company of North America, so we moved from New York to Detroit when I was halfway through the sixth grade.

Dad knew how to have fun, but took himself very seriously and was extremely goal-directed. He played golf at Orchid Lake Country Club, learned to ski at age 45, and joined a curling club with my mother (that odd winter sport that uses "stones" and appears to the untutored eye to be a combination of shuffleboard and housecleaning).

When I came home for vacations from college, and later from medical school, he would always come alone to pick me up at the airport. We'd shake hands. He'd get my bags and then on the drive home ask me what distinguished the painting of Vermeer from Monet; how did Sartre influence existentialism; how was I doing with my French and organic chemistry? We didn't talk about how I liked school, if I had any friends, or what I did in my spare time. It was mostly intellectual curiosity about subjects, never "Are you getting any playing time on the team? Have you met any girls? Are you happy?" In medical school, he wanted to know how the blood circulated. What was the endocrine system? What was the purpose of the pineal gland? He never asked if I worried about missing a diagnosis, making a mistake, or if it was hard to see people sick and dying. There were things he could have asked me, but there were also many things I could have told him.

Perhaps the best way to describe our relationship is to recount the details of a family trip to Alaska. The vacation was organized by my father and included my mother, my sister, Janet, and me. It took Dad six months to plan the itinerary and arrange the details, during which time Eddie Bauer and L.L. Bean catalogues were scattered everywhere in our den, along with maps, brochures, and various pieces of information from *National Geographic* and other sources about Alaska and the Yukon Territory. He purchased flannel shirts, hunting boots, special khaki pants, fishing waders, a fly rod, a fishing cap, bandanas, and a Gortex jacket with a removable vest. The rest of us packed more casually: jeans, socks, some tennis shoes, T-shirts, sweatshirts, a wind breaker, a baseball hat. Our plans were to fly from Detroit to Seattle, where a Lincoln Continental Mark III car was waiting. We would drive to a ferry and travel up the inland passage to Skagway, then drive the Alcan Highway to Whitehorse in the Yukon Territory, then continue on to Dawson, Anchorage, and Fairbanks.

When we arrived at the luggage carrier in Seattle to pick up our bags, Dad's enormous new suitcase was conspicuously absent. The conveyor belt turned and turned. After thirty minutes there was only one item left on the belt: a small mammal cage with a mesh front and a handle on top. Inside was a snarling black ferret, a type of weasel. Dad gently lifted the cage and checked the tag. It matched his claim check. He carried the ferret in its cage to the baggage agent who was ill-prepared for the ensuing tirade from this high school All-American Phi Beta Kappa Harvard English major former lieutenant in the United States Navy holding aloft a snarling ferret and assuring the agent this angry mammal played no part in his preparation for a two-week family vacation in Alaska.

After checking by phone (no computers in those days), it was discovered the owner of the ferret was equally upset that his beloved pet was in Alaska and not where he belonged, in Santiago, Chile. Ironically, Santiago was the very city my paternal grandfather had sent lengthy letters in Spanish to his pen pal. I doubt if the subject of ferrets was ever discussed during those years of correspondence, but life is full of irony. More to the point, the Chilean holding my father's Eddie Bauer deluxe leather trim suitcase with brass fixtures and easy-glide wheels (a new invention) refused to release the luggage until he gained possession of the ferret. The agent assured my father his gear would be waiting for him in Skagway, and the airline made a good-will compensation of $100.00, with which he purchased socks, underwear, and an inexpensive blue and white striped seersucker robe. Everything else he required was in his suitcase and could wait. The socks, underwear, and robe were purchased at a Sears and Roebucks not far from the Seattle airport. His business suit and shirt were dry-cleaned (a one-hour special) while he waited, wrapped in the cotton robe.

Finally, we drove the huge Lincoln Continental Mark III onto the ferry and enjoyed a leisurely and scenic cruise to Skagway. Upon arrival, however, Dad discovered his bags were not in Skagway, but had been taken to our hotel in Whitehorse by a Ford dealer wishing to impress my father with his initiative. "Initiative" was not the word chosen by my father to describe this well-meaning nincompoop. As we headed out to the Alcan Highway, Dad, at the helm of a V8 280 horsepower fuel-injected Lincoln Continental Mark III, was on the verge of lunacy. He was a well-dressed lunatic, but one who had the stern look of displeasure I had seen many times before, first as a mildly intoxicated two-year-old and later at intervals over the years.

We all knew to be quiet, no questions. Mom tried to diffuse the tension. She commented that during the Alaskan summer it never got dark. The sky was clear. She spotted moose and turned on the radio to a country-western station mixed with static. Dad pointedly reached over and turned the radio off. I sat in the backseat behind Mom and next to my sister, Janet. I could see my father's jaw muscles working, his hands gripping the steering wheel with unnecessary tension, especially allowing for the new innovation of "finger touch" power steering now standard on luxury Ford Motor Company products.

Then we rounded a curve and were met by twenty or thirty cars and trucks, a tourist bus, and three semi-trucks all parked in a line, a wilderness traffic jam. Dad got out to assess the situation, a Ford executive in full business attire—gaberdine suit, starched white shirt, striped tie, polished dress shoes, and dark socks with garters—walking casually but purposefully, just as he might have strolled into a board meeting with Edsel Ford and Lee Iococca, except now he was passing men in trucks dressed for the wilderness in flannel shirts and jeans likely purchased from the Sears and Roebuck store where Dad had obtained his underwear and robe.

Beyond the back-up of the trucks and cars was a bridge. I could see a truck driver calmly talking with my father. The bridge was built with railroad ties and rebar, but it was now splintered and partially collapsed in the center. A trucker had called the highway department on his CB. They said they would arrive in four to six hours. They had no idea how long it would take to repair the bridge. It would be best to return to Skagway. My father listened intently, analyzing this information as if a junior marketing executive was pitching him an idea for a new ad campaign. He didn't speak, but took in everything. Then he motioned to our car. Mom got out, but he waved her off and signaled for me. I met him by the bridge. He asked me to walk across the bridge with him for an inspection. I was entering seventh grade and did okay in math, but had not yet studied civil engineering. The bridge didn't seem that bad. I jumped up and down a few times. Nothing gave, but, of course, I only weighed 150 pounds. The bridge was about thirty yards wide with a twenty-foot drop to the water below, clear cold mountain water loaded with salmon and trout. "Well, it looks okay to me, Dad."

That was all he wanted to hear, all he needed. I think he'd already made up his mind. His fishing gear and belongings were waiting in Whitehorse on the other side of the bridge. It was a three-hour drive back to Skagway. For him the decision was clear. Mom, Janet, and I moved the luggage from the car to the other side of the bridge and waited.

I will never know why all of those other adults in line didn't restrain my father. Maybe it was the way he walked; confident, head up, in a business suit, a lunatic, a goal-driven maniac on the verge of a breakdown. They remained silent and kept their distance. Dad drove to the edge of the bridge and studied the landmarks. Then he put the enormous 1956 Lincoln Continental Mark III in reverse gear and backed slowly 200 yards up the dusty Alcan Highway. It was 8 p.m. in July, clear and light. The only sounds were the distant idling of my dad's car, a breeze rustling the alder trees on the river bank, the soft buzz of mosquitoes, and the call of a western flycatcher.

Then there was an eruption of dirt and spinning wheels, a confirmation of the TV advertisements that a Lincoln Continental can achieve an acceleration from zero to 70 in eight seconds. The sedan hit the bridge at 75 miles an hour and launched like Thelma and Louise, like Evil Knievel in a business suit—all business. I could see my father's intense eyes through the windshield, wide open, that look that made me want to get straight As, win awards, shoot the winning basket, suck it up, go for it. Men lined the edge of the road beside their vehicles, speechless, the silence broken only by the cracking sound of wood and railroad ties dropping into the water below and then gently floating downstream. The entire center section of the bridge had collapsed after dad made it safely across. Did anyone get out to check our license number? I hoped not. We loaded up and drove off. Dad got his gear in Whitehorse and we had a great trip. He was a hero. What a man! He had set a goal and achieved it.

One summer, almost fifty years after our family trip to Alaska, I drove with my wife over a similar bridge in British Columbia. When I told her the story of our family trip, she was shocked. How could my father do such a thing? What if the bridge had cracked a few seconds earlier? My father would have hit the far bank at 75 miles an hour, the Lincoln Continental a flaming inferno, my mother an instant widow with two orphans 400 miles from anywhere, standing helpless with suitcases on the far side of a broken bridge in the Yukon Territory. Furthermore, he had asked a seventh grade boy to endorse his decision. How reckless. How imprudent. How insane. She was right of course. All of these years I thought of my dad as a hero, but now I saw he could also be viewed as a selfish, reckless, irresponsible husband and father more intent on getting his gear and completing our itinerary than considering the welfare of his family. I had never thought of it that way.

And sometimes that's my problem, too. I would like to think that I am selfless, caring, and rational, but in many ways I'm like my dad, a goal-driven overachiever, seeing the trees, missing the forest, more in touch with things of the mind and less with things of the heart. I remember all of the talks about Vermeer and Sartre and the endocrine system and the pineal gland. I never discussed simple things with him—like the warning signs of a heart attack.

A few years after our Alaskan vacation my father returned from a golfing trip. His suitcase was too heavy, his arm and shoulder ached. "Damn suitcase." He began to sweat. "Boy, I need to cut down on my smoking." He was nauseated and then vomited. "Never could stomach airline food." Shortly after he arrived home he collapsed. Mom called 9-1-1. I was told that an ambulance took him to the William Beaumont Hospital. This was before advanced CPR, intravenous lidocaine, cardioversion, and thrombolytics were given in the ambulance by paramedics.

At the very same moment, even allowing for the time difference between Michigan and New Mexico, I was in a hospital emergency room in Albuquerque treating another man with an acute myocardial infarction. In all of our conversations, I had never told my father the basic signs of a pending heart attack. I also never told him how much I loved him, respected him, and wanted to be like him. As I administered the treatments given too late to my father, my patient stabilized as my father's blood pressure dropped and he lost consciousness, his heart fibrillating. Attempts at resuscitation with repeated electric shocks and assisted ventilation were of no help. He was essentially dead on arrival in the ER while my patient was stabilized and transferred to the cardiac care unit.

My mother was too upset to speak. A neighbor and good friend of our family called that afternoon to tell me my father had died. Then, I imagined my father approaching a bridge at 75 miles per hour. Airborne, he made it across the river, but his trajectory was too high. He continued to sail into the gray Alaskan sky and beyond, forever and ever, while I watched, helpless, standing with my mother and my sister and our suitcases.

# FRANKLIN WOODY

In the introduction to these stories, a postscript is defined as an added remark at the end of a letter. This final chapter is a postscript from me, at the end of a book-length letter to future physicians and others. It is, by no means, an afterthought. Franklin's true name will not be spoken, according to Navajo customs regarding the deceased.

I met Franklin Woody, a third-grade student at Dilkon Elementary School, when he was an eight-year-old aspiring Indian hoop dancer. At the time, I was a new, twenty-seven-year-old doctor, responsible for the health and welfare of my patients after completing four years of medical school and a one-year internal medicine internship. I had no experience with ambulatory pediatrics. The memory of my encounter with Franklin at the school clinic on that Friday in 1971, the day after Thanksgiving, would remain with me throughout forty-five years of medical practice.

First, a bit of history. Even today, doctors called general medical officers serve in the military and other federal health programs. They assume the full responsibility of patient care after only a one-year internship. Instead of being drafted for the war in Vietnam, I was permitted to serve as a general medical officer in the Commissioned Corps of the United States Public Health Service (USPHS), Indian Health Service (IHS), to satisfy my military obligation. In the IHS I was fortunate to associate with some of the most intelligent, well-trained, compassionate, dedicated physicians I have known. All four doctors at the Winslow Indian Hospital working with me were general medical officers with one-year internships: internal medicine, pediatric, surgical, and rotating. Our diverse training experiences and clinical inexperience made sure we constantly consulted with one another. We were all in our mid to late twenties, as were most doctors at IHS hospitals and clinics across America during and after the Vietnam war. Board certified specialists were available for consultation at referral centers in Gallup, New Mexico; Albuquerque, New Mexico; Phoenix, Arizona; and other medical centers mainly in western states with large populations of Native Americans. Years later, after residency, I was appointed Chief of Medicine at the Phoenix Indian Medical Center.

Healthcare for Native Americans was originally provided by treaties between Indian tribes and the U.S. War Department, serving mainly to protect army forts and white settlers from attack or exposure to communicable diseases as these new Americans encroached westward into Indian territories, where white settlers exercised their perceived right to "Manifest Destiny." In 1849 Indian healthcare was transferred to the Department of the Interior, whose mission was to protect America's "natural resources." Healthcare and education were administered by the Bureau of Indian Affairs, where the principal objective was to homogenize Native American languages and customs to blend in with the dominant white culture. Finally, in 1926, Indian healthcare was assumed by the Commissioned Corps (CC) of the USPHS, a branch of the Department of Health and Human Services. The CC was designed to better serve the needs of First Nation Peoples, most of whom lived on reservations and in rural areas. The IHS continues to serve the health needs of Native Americans today, though some tribes now fund and administer their own health programs without government subsidies.

When I examined Franklin Woody at the school clinic, Paula Gertler, the school nurse, told me that several of Franklin's classmates had recently been treated for streptococcal pharyngitis, a highly contagious condition. Franklin had been ill for three days and met some of the criteria for a strep infection: red pharynx, slightly enlarged tonsils, fever of 101 degrees, body aches, and general malaise. Cervical lymph nodes were not enlarged. There was no skin rash or nuchal rigidity. He did, in retrospect, appear to be more ill than the physical findings suggested. Perhaps I was misled by the history of strep infections among his classmates. Things might have turned out differently had I honored my suspicion, my intuition, that Franklin Woody suffered from a more serious illness. I was familiar with the Hippocratic approach to treatment, but had not yet acquired sufficient experience to apply these principals to patient care, the art of medicine. An early diagnosis is fraught with danger—unfamiliar, blurred margins often mislead an unsuspecting doctor to exclude from consideration alternative and perhaps more serious conditions.

I was on solo call at the hospital for the holiday weekend. Things would be quiet. There were no rodeos in town. Furthermore, Thanksgiving (and Columbus Day), are not among the favorite holidays celebrated by Native Americans. Before I left Franklin, I swabbed a throat culture and told Paula, the school nurse, I would call back the next day with the results. Franklin was encouraged to increase his fluid intake, use ibuprofen for his fever, and rest. After twenty-four hours I called Paula with the "good news": the pharyngeal culture was negative for beta-hemolytic streptococci. She then informed me that Franklin had just returned to the school clinic. He was confused and lethargic. A severe headache had developed overnight. He was en route to our hospital in the school van.

Before he arrived, however, a thirty-six-year-old diabetic woman entered the emergency room in active labor. She had received no prenatal care. The woman had six previous vaginal deliveries, a grand multipara, but her abdomen seemed unusually distended. Did she have polyhydramnious, twin fetuses, or an abnormal fetal position? An x-ray confirmed the breech presentation of a ten-pound fetus. Normally this condition would have been detected earlier by ultrasound and she would have been sent for a C-section, but she had received no prenatal care. In the midst of this obstetric crisis, the nursing staff alerted me that Franklin Woody had arrived in perilous condition, but I could not abandon the mother with a partially delivered baby. After ninety minutes of difficult labor, only the cyanotic legs and feet of the unborn baby presented to the world. In addition, the umbilical cord was now compressed around the infant's neck. The fetal monitor beeped distress. There was no choice but to extract the baby forcefully from the birth canal, breaking both clavicles and dislocating the shoulders. At birth the APGAR score was an ominous three. After administration of oxygen, vigorous massage, and stimulation, the child began to cry. His color pinked up and spontaneous respirations ensued. Later, I could repair the mother's traumatized birth canal and perform a more detailed examination of the newborn. Fortunately, there was no permanent injury to the brachial plexus or cranium of the child.

I then rushed from the delivery room, just having witnessed the beginning of a new life, to check on Franklin, hoping that I had not forfeited his right to life. He was delirious and tachypneic with a temperature of 103 degrees, blood pressure of 60/30, and a weak, rapid pulse. Ashen skin was punctuated with a purple, blotchy, purpuric rash. The nurses had started an IV and begun oxygen supplementation by mask. Corticosteroids, antibiotics, and vasopressors were administered through the IV line. A urinary catheter was inserted and a lumbar puncture performed. The cerebrospinal fluid (CSF) was turbid and under increased pressure. All body fluids were cultured and subsequently grew Neisseria meningitidis. Gram stain of the CSF teemed with leukocytes and the gram negative diplococci typical of this deadly bacterium. Franklin now had full blown Waterhouse-Friderichsen Syndrome: adrenal failure, and overwhelming gram negative sepsis. He died thirty minutes later. Had I given empiric therapy with LA Bicillin for presumed streptococcal pharyngitis twenty-four hours earlier at the school clinic, he might have survived, although penicillin penetrates the blood brain barrier poorly. More importantly, I had not yet acquired the clinical judgement to determine that he was severely ill despite the relative paucity of his initial physical findings. He needed hospital admission for further testing and observation. I should have brought him directly back to the hospital with me on Friday.

There is no substitute for experience, no matter how well-trained the physician. Learning the art of medicine takes time. The "retrospectoscope" does not exist. A poor outcome can only advise our future decisions with patient management. Given time, we refine our skills. Looking back only helps to remind us of the formidable responsibility a physician undertakes when rendering care to another human being.

Forgive me, Franklin. I am so sorry. May God embrace you. May He bless us all.

# Biographies

## Author

Dr. Fisher was born in Boston, Massachusetts, in 1943. He is a graduate of Cranbrook School, Princeton University, and Columbia University College of Physicians and Surgeons. He interned at Harlem Hospital and completed a two year medical residency at the University of New Mexico School of Medicine, Bernalillo County Medical Center. He has worked for the Department of State, Indian Health Service, and in private group practice. In 1974, he was elected as a Fellow of the American College of Physicians.

Dr. Fisher is married and lives in Phoenix, Arizona. Now retired, he mentors first- and second-year students at the University of Arizona College of Medicine. He is also an avid bird watcher and amateur entomologist. This is his second book.

## Artist

Tim Janicki earned a master's degree in education from Drake University and is a graduate of the University of Wisconsin–Milwaukee with a bachelor of fine arts. He taught public school in Iowa for thirty years. Now retired, Tim works in soft pastel, ink, and acrylic, doing landscapes, classic cars, and portraits as his main subject matter. He has completed many commissioned artworks and several mural projects. His work is found in many private collections. Tim is a member of several art organizations in the Phoenix area, and is currently serving as president of the Vanguard Artists in Northwest Phoenix Valley. This is the third book he has illustrated.

# ACKNOWLEDGEMENTS

I wish to express my sincere gratitude to Vicky Thomas, owner of "Doc Talk" Transcription Services, for tirelessly recording the original manuscript; Lucy W. Rollin, Professor Emeritus of English, Clemson University, for editing the manuscript; and especially to my daughter, Meredith Fisher, for helping with revisions and circulation with good humor and patience. Finally, thanks to Luka Fisher for creative ideas in marketing this book.